MORE FISH TALES

Paul Salmon is one of the champions of the Australian Football League. He played for 18 years for Essendon and Hawthorn, retiring at the end of 2000, and made a successful comeback with the Bombers in 2002 under his old mentor Kevin Sheedy. Paul's career spanned 20 seasons and 324 games, and included five Premierships (two day, three night), three All-Australian selections, two club Best & Fairests, a Tassie medal and the Michael Tuck Medal. He represented Victoria 14 times in State of Origin football.

Paul has various business interests and is a director of Journey Events Travel, which specialises in event travel packaging, and Work@Play, a corporate communications and entertainment company. His media commitments include co-hosting *Sportsworld* with Johanna Griggs, appearing as a regular member of *Rex Hunt's Footy Panel* and presenting sports wraps on *Sunrise*, all on the Seven Network, and football commentary on ABC radio. Paul, who was Victoria's 'Father of the Year' in 2000, is married and has three children. His previous books are his autobiography, *The Big Fish* (2001), and *Fish Tales* (2002).

Also by Paul Salmon

The Big Fish
Fish Tales

MORE FISH TALES

Favourite yarns from a footballing life

PAUL SALMON

VIKING
an imprint of
PENGUIN BOOKS

Viking

Published by the Penguin Group
Penguin Books Australia Ltd
250 Camberwell Road, Camberwell, Victoria 3124, Australia
Penguin Books Ltd
80 Strand, London WC2R 0RL, England
Penguin Putnam Inc.
375 Hudson Street, New York, New York 10014, USA
Penguin Books, a division of Pearson Canada
10 Alcorn Avenue, Toronto, Ontario, Canada M4V 3B2
Penguin Books (NZ) Ltd
Cnr Rosedale and Airborne Roads, Albany, Auckland, New Zealand
Penguin Books (South Africa) (Pty) Ltd
24 Sturdee Avenue, Rosebank, Johannesburg 2196, South Africa
Penguin Books India (P) Ltd
11, Community Centre, Panchsheel Park, New Delhi 110 017, India

First published by Penguin Books Australia Ltd 2003

10 9 8 7 6 5 4 3 2 1

Copyright © Paul Salmon 2003

The moral right of the author has been asserted

All rights reserved. Without limiting the rights under copyright reserved above, no part of this publication may be reproduced, stored in or introduced into a retrieval system, or transmitted, in any form or by any means (electronic, mechanical, photocopying, recording or otherwise), without the prior written permission of both the copyright owner and the above publisher of this book.

Design by Brad Maxwell, Penguin Design Studio
Cover photography © Tim de Neefe
Typeset in 12/14 pt Stempel Garamond by Midland Typesetters, Maryborough, Victoria
Printed and bound in Australia by McPherson's Printing Group, Maryborough, Victoria

National Library of Australia
Cataloguing-in-Publication data:

Salmon, Paul, 1965– .
More fish tales.

ISBN 0 670 04129 7.

1. Salmon, Paul, 1965– . 2. Australian football players – Biography.
3. Australian football – Anecdotes. I. Title.

796.336092

www.penguin.com.au

To all the people who contributed to making my football career about much more than getting a kick. You know who you are — you've either already made it into my previous books, or you've been praying there would never be more 'Fish tales'!

CONTENTS

Acknowledgements ix

Introduction 1

Part 1 Footy trips
Pizza 7
Broadway 11
Pet 16

Part 2 Joys of youth
Price of fame 21
Legends 25
Space 29
Ruckman 32
Trust me 35

Part 3 Match-day madness
Coach's box 39
Sheeds 45
Horsin' around 48
Official nonsense 52
In the mood 55
Dice of life 61

Part 4 Mates rates
Follow your dream 67
Only T.D. 74
Big break 77
On the nose 80
Gotta go! 82

Part 5 Unsung heroes
Bomber backbone 87
Balloons 91
Property 93
Ace 98
Microwave 101
The psych 104
Touchy-feely 109
Minder 113

Part 6 Telly tales
Sound effects 119
Simon and Lou 121
Big screen 124

Part 7 Big occasions
Shadow-boxing 131
Procession 135
Faking it 138
Piles 141
Like gold 143

Part 8 Livelihood
Tour guide 147
Foot in mouth 150
Bricks and mortar 153
The syndicate 157

Part 9 Comeback
Twilight zone 163
Routine 167
Last hurrah 170

ACKNOWLEDGEMENTS

A very big thank-you to the man who helped bring this book to life, Brad McKenzie. For Brad, nothing was ever a problem and everything was a pleasure (did I pay him too much?). They say Shane Warne is the 'Sheik of Tweak', but when it comes to the written word, it's Brad who's the Sheik.

Thanks again to the team at Penguin, in particular Katie Purvis and Bob Sessions for inviting me to write another book and for all their help and support along the way. I'm so glad you guys encouraged me to do it, and that I got to work with such professionals.

I hope my children experience as much fulfilment in their lives as I have in mine. Their reaction to my writing another book was similar to the one they had when they had friends over for a swim recently and I came out to the pool in a pair of Speedos: 'Please, Dad, noooo!'

So, to my wife, Jo, and kids, Leah, Lachlan and Sian, thank you – your love, support and belief in me are what make every day of my life worth living.

INTRODUCTION

I THINK WE try too hard to overcomplicate things sometimes, so my policy has always been the old 'K.I.S.S. principle': keep it simple, stupid. There was nothing complex about deciding to make a comeback to football with Essendon in 2002 and there is certainly nothing complex about *More Fish Tales*. I've had a ball throughout my football career doing what I love, with people I've loved doing it with – playing footy, that is!

I decided to write *More Fish Tales* after getting a rare chance to go back to playing our great game, when I least expected it. It was further confirmation of what took retirement for me to really appreciate: that you tend to miss the people more than the footy. So when I was invited by Penguin to head back to the computer and document some more yarns from a life in Aussie Rules, I saw it as a chance to share more of the moments that have made my life unique in so many ways. Writing this book was a lot of fun. My previous book, *Fish Tales*, was a collection of stories that flowed very easily, but this one had me thinking more about what makes a club tick and the characters involved in the everyday life of a footballer. I think anyone who has played or been involved with football, at any level, will be able to relate to *More Fish Tales*.

The only complicated thing about my comeback last year was how to make it happen after settling into retirement. A wife and three kids who had just started to get used to having me around, business commitments and media contracts all made it a little tough to pull off, but I couldn't believe how much support I got from everyone concerned. With everything sorted, I thought that one more year out of my life wasn't much in the overall picture.

I was genuinely excited about taking the risk of putting myself up for ridicule by coming back to play footy with the Bombers. Kevin Sheedy and James Hird had made it hard to say no, telling me of their desire to have a successful year and the role I might be able to play in it. Of course, I would have to set about re-marking my territory – not by urinating against a wall, but with the odd bad joke. That way, I knew I'd get my space.

It was a year full of challenges for the Bombers, with some of the team's best seriously injured. Yet we saw young players with big futures present themselves to the football world. It's always the way with adversity: people get opportunities and some make the most of them.

I don't regret in any way the decision to come back, as it was yet another case of saying I will not die wondering. I can't believe how lucky I am to have played for both Essendon and Hawthorn, and how fortunate I am to have stayed for so long as a player in the game I love.

I'll never forget the day Kevin Sheedy asked me if I could come back and help him out, six years after letting me go as a 31-year-old hack. Returning to Essendon after six years away was like being in a time warp. The look was different, but the feel was the same. I felt like a kid again as I attempted to train my body and mind for one last year of football at the top level. It was comforting in a lot of ways that the critical people behind any possible successful comeback for me were still there: Sheeds, Doc Reid, Bruce Connor (club physio) and some old mates in Hirdy, Steve Alessio, Matthew Lloyd, Joe

Introduction

Misiti, Dustin Fletcher and Mark Mercuri. New faces like assistant coach John Quinn, football manager Matthew Drain and CEO Peter Jackson were also key players in a year when both me and the footy club were putting a bit on the line.

The first time I put the red and black on for a training session I couldn't help but feel a little guilty because of the close identification I had developed with Hawthorn. I had to remind myself constantly that I was helping out some old mates and trying to win a premiership, which was possible, at the very least, given the list at Essendon's disposal. Seeing as how it was most unlikely that Hawthorn would be in need of my services, I reasoned that one year out of my life to attempt every footballer's dream was worth any perceived risk. The size of the challenge was intoxicating and the chance of finally being an Essendon ruckman for a year was way too attractive. It had been the desire to ruck that led me to Hawthorn in the first place. The irony.

Football is a funny game, they say, and it is, but mostly in hindsight. To survive and prosper in any walk of life there's one ingredient you need above all else: self-belief. Maybe I did compromise my association with Hawthorn by going back to Essendon, and I apologise to those Hawk fans who think so, but when all is said and done, I loved playing football when I was nine years old and nothing was different when I was thirty-seven. Hawthorn changed my life for the better, and for that reason I will always be a Hawthorn man.

In fact, not a lot changes in football. It doesn't matter what you do to the bricks and mortar – clubs are built on the character of those who exist within them. It's people who make football clubs, and Hawthorn and Essendon have some of the best. Having said that, it's time to reveal some of the things that make those people memorable. So sit back with a refreshment in one hand and *More Fish Tales* in the other, and join me on another journey into the world of AFL football.

PART 1
FOOTY TRIPS

PIZZA

END-OF-SEASON club trips are very similar to government conferences in that they are always held somewhere far away and slightly exotic. You will never hear of a football team going to, say, Broken Hill or Mount Isa for their end of year trip. I have been fortunate enough to go to Noumea, Fiji, Bali, Tokyo, England and the USA.

One thing all footballers hold sacred about the end-of-season trip is the unwritten law, 'What happens on the footy trip stays on the footy trip'. (Actually, now that I have written it, I guess it's not unwritten any more, is it?) One of the reasons it is held sacred is because sometimes things happen on trips that could prove pretty embarrassing if they were ever revealed back home.

One such event occurred on my first trip to America, when I found myself in a relatively compromising position with a teammate. And it's not what you're thinking! It was way back in 1984, when a hungry Peter Bradbury (a Premiership player that year) and I were standing out the front of a San Francisco nightclub at two o'clock in the morning. We decided to catch a cab, thinking a cabbie would know all the good places to eat. We had both watched enough American television to know how to hail a cab, and Pete strode confidently into the middle of the street and put his arm out.

Footy trips

Unfortunately, he'd forgotten to take into account that in the States they drive on the other side of the road, and he was almost run over as cars took evasive action to avoid him. On a positive note, a cab did stop. We jumped in and asked the cabbie to take us somewhere we could get a good feed, then leaned back to enjoy the ride. We went about 200 metres before he stopped and pointed to a pizza restaurant on our left. 'There you go, guys. That'll be ten bucks.'

Just as we'd seen people do on the telly, Pete peeled off a ten-dollar bill, plus a dollar tip, and threw them on to the driver's seat, and we climbed out, thanking him. If you've ever been to the States you'll know that all their banknotes are the same size and colour. And if you're a bit drunk, it's easy to make a mistake. Pete had got the one-dollar tip spot on, but the ten-dollar bill he'd peeled off and thrown down was actually a $100 bill. He didn't realise until we were just about to walk into the pizza place. You know how, on American shows, there's always so much traffic no one goes anywhere? That's not true at 2 a.m. That cab was off like a shot and out of sight by the time we turned around.

It was then we noticed that most of the people on the street were men, and the vast majority were holding hands. Pete and I were stuck in the gayest area of the gayest city in America. We looked at each other and said, 'Well, here we are – may as well make the most of it,' and went into the pizza joint. The whole place went silent and heads turned our way as we walked in together, obviously out of place. We were both dressed in Levis, sneakers and Exacto T-shirts and, in hindsight, should have put a little more thought into our wardrobe, because it seemed every gay guy in the place was dressed the same.

Pete and I didn't know where to look. All we knew was that we were getting checked out pretty closely. We sat down quickly and grabbed a menu. I mentioned to Pete that if we got out of this alive I would never openly ogle a woman again.

Pizza

A guy with a huge handlebar moustache bounded over and asked for our order. Pete ordered a large Hawaiian and the waiter turned to him, smiled knowingly and said, 'I'll see if we have one out the back.'

Not wanting to fall into the double-entendre trap, I looked the waiter straight in the eye and confidently ordered one with the lot. He came back with, 'That doesn't surprise me at all.' He didn't even blink; it was almost like he was willing me to order exactly that. This guy was good – very good. He wandered off to the kitchen (well, to be honest, he sashayed off like Mr Humphries from *Are You Being Served?*).

Pete decided we should make the most of our situation and suggested that we pretend to be a couple so as not to draw attention to ourselves. I slid my hand across the table to take his and blew him a kiss. Pete froze – obviously he hadn't thought I'd embrace his idea so quickly.

Our pizzas arrived, with the waiter saying to Pete, 'Sorry, sir, we didn't have a big Hawaiian out the back. I hope this will be okay.' He then turned to me, put my pizza down and grabbed his groin, saying, 'And as for you, sir, I have one with the lot, just as you requested.' I have never eaten a pizza so fast in my life. Had Guinness been there, I have no doubt I would have made it straight into the book.

We got up to leave and conversation in the restaurant stopped again. The guy in the booth behind us turned as we were getting up and put his hand on my shoulder. 'Going so soon? Why are you in such a hurry? Come and join us,' he said, patting the vinyl seat next to him. I had no idea what to do or say. 'Where are you from, big boy?' he asked. I stood there with my mouth open – not a good look in a gay pizza barn, I can tell you.

Pete came in beautifully. He grabbed me on the arse – with perhaps just a little too much familiarity – and said, 'He's mine, mate,' then we made a dash for the street. Talk about a couple of nerds at the cool kids' party.

We grabbed a cab back to the hotel and promised one another that the experience would remain with us, as the rest of the boys might not believe that we'd only found our way to the pizza place by accident.

It was a bonding experience for Pete and me. However, I did feel I had to warn him that although he certainly knew how to grab arse, he'd better not try it again or I'd do what the waiter couldn't, and organise a big Hawaiian to pay him a visit.

BROADWAY

IN 1997 THE end-of-season trip for the Hawks was to America, and one afternoon I found myself wandering the streets of New York with Jason Dunstall and Skippy, the guy who used to place the witches' hats at training. Also with us was one of our most generous sponsors. For fear of retribution I can't name this sponsor, so let's just call him 'Sonny'.

We had taken in a day of sightseeing, including the Empire State Building, Times Square and the Statue of Liberty. On the way we had also gone to the FAO Schwarz toy store, where I had loaded up on presents for the kids. (If any toy-store representatives are reading this book, may I make a suggestion? In all your stores you should put a 'Presents for Parents who Feel Bad that They Didn't Bring Their Kids Along, and Hope This Toy Will Make Up for It' section. Sales would increase dramatically. Make it stuff that can fit in a suitcase and looks more expensive than it actually costs, and you are on the way to a small fortune. Advertise it in those booklets you get in hotel rooms and in in-flight magazines, and the money will roll in. Mark my words.)

So here we were, tired, thirsty and me laden down with gifts, walking down Fifth Avenue on our way back to the hotel with four hours to spare to get ready to go to a Broadway show. Jason suggested that perhaps we should pop into a bar for a drink. We had plenty of time up our sleeve, so we all agreed. The bar we chose was Mickey Mantle's, just off Fifth Avenue, right next to the Ritz Carlton hotel. All the staff there wear baseball gear featuring the famous number 7, and there's all sorts of memorabilia adorning the walls. The staff were very welcoming and we quickly found ourselves sitting on stools at the bar. One of the reasons we were so welcome was that we were the only ones there.

We had a beer each, then another, then another, and pretty soon an hour had gone by. As the beer flowed, so did the stories, each one getting taller and taller, as they do. I checked my watch, did some mental calculations and decided it would be a good time to call home. Turns out it was two in the morning in Melbourne, but I'm sure my wife, Jo, was rapt to hear from me. The reason she was so short on the phone was probably to allow me to get back to my mates – she's very understanding.

Phone call out of the way, get back to my mates I did. By now it was 5 p.m. and the office workers in the area had knocked off and started to make their way into the bar. The atmosphere had lifted five notches and we had gone from being charming Aussie tourists to devils from down under. And somehow, during my short but sweet conversation home, beer had been replaced by colourful drinks in very small glasses.

Six p.m. rolled around and Sonny declared that if we were going to make the show we should get going. We called him soft, then said it was fine if he wanted to go – we would finish our drinks, maybe have one more, and meet him at the hotel.

Sonny swung his feet to the floor and attempted to stand. I say 'attempted' because he looked like a baby giraffe taking its first steps. Undeterred, and obviously eager to make it to the show, he started to crawl on his hands and knees to the door. In America everybody minds their own business and, as far as service goes, nothing is too much trouble. Hence, all the patrons in the bar just looked the other way and the doorman didn't even flinch. He just held the door open and said, 'Have a good evening, sir,' as Sonny crawled his way into peak-hour pedestrian traffic.

I thought, after a minute or so (in hindsight it felt like a minute or so, but time was moving through molasses by then and it was probably longer), that perhaps I should go out and help Sonny find his way home. What made me think I was in any better condition than him I'll never know. I stood up from my stool and immediately felt a little woozy. Have you seen *American Gigolo*, where Richard Gere does his stomach exercises by hanging upside down from his calves in his doorway? That's how I felt – like I'd been upside down for hours. My head knew where it wanted to go, but my feet were having trouble doing as they were told. I stood for a second, swaying like one of the Lego towers my son used to build, then just toppled over.

Fate smiled on me that day, because through sheer luck there was a table next to me. A couple eating potato wedges and enjoying a quiet beer were soon joined by a very drunk Aussie lying in their salsa trying to apologise and at the same time laughing like a drain. Jason and Skippy were no help at all, and even if they had wanted to help, they probably couldn't have left their stools, so they just sat there laughing.

It became apparent very quickly that in America they're very concerned about litigation. The bar manager and two of the staff came over straight away and helped me up, all the time asking if I was hurt in any way. Of course I wasn't hurt – I was drunk! If I'd been sober I probably would have broken a major bone. In fact, I was so drunk I could have walked in front of a bus and not been hurt. Anyway, the bar manager and staff apologised for putting the table in a place where someone might trip over it. They then offered to supply a round of drinks for the three of us to make up for the mistake. It's often said that

Americans aren't good with irony, and this was a classic example – surely it was the drink that had caused the incident in the first place. Then again, who was I to refuse their offer? If it helped them feel better, I was happy to oblige.

Very quickly another three drinks appeared on the bar. While Jason and Skippy got stuck into them, I remembered that the whole reason I'd left the stool was to check on Sonny. I ventured outside to find him trying to use the wall of the Ritz Carlton for leverage as he struggled to get vertical. I staggered back to my stool at the bar and, downing my drink, said to the boys, 'He's gone, fellas. So drunk he can't stand up.' Believe me, I was in a position to know. 'Weak as piss,' Jason said.

After a few more drinks – just so our hosts didn't feel bad, you understand – we decided that if we were going to make the show we'd better find our way back to the hotel. The three of us got up and, without a word of a lie, when we got to the door the entire bar cheered. The manager even presented me with a complimentary Mickey Mantle T-shirt and cap!

Bung (Jason) decided we should travel back to the hotel in a style befitting the conquerors of Fifth Avenue. (Well, that was what we wanted to believe we were.) He suggested that one of the row of horse-and-carriage operators across the street would appreciate our custom and we should make our way over there to secure a ride home. To be honest, the suggestion probably went more like this: 'Why don't we hijack one of those carriages and take it back to our room so the boys can joyride it around the hotel?' And Skippy and I probably answered, 'Yeah, why not!'

Trying to cross a New York street in peak hour without all your senses is arguably a little risky, but we weren't applying a lot of rationality to our decision-making at that point. We made it safely, so I can only guess that Lady Luck smiled on us big-time that day. Or that Bung must have decided to practise his traffic-cop routine. I suppose I may never know.

Broadway

As I had left every last cent in the 'tip' jar back at the bar, I assumed Bung would have the fare covered. Rule number 1 on a footy trip: you can't trust anyone! We got in a carriage and soon pulled into the foyer entry, to see our group gathered ready for their excursion to Broadway. Thank goodness they were there, because between the three of us we didn't have a cracker to pay the driver with, and doing a runner wasn't even an option: we would have been hard pressed to do a walker. I don't know who paid for our ride. We had no hope of getting to the show and decided it might be prudent if we just took ourselves off to bed. It was no doubt my earliest night on a footy trip ever.

You'll be relieved to know that all the presents made it home in one piece. I do hope the kids appreciated what I went through to get their gifts back to Australia. We left a little piece of ourselves behind in New York, as evidenced by the fact that Sonny returned some three years later to the scene of our big day out, Mickey Mantle's. Upon entering he was greeted with 'Hey! Aren't you one of those Aussie guys who were here a few years back?'

Sonny stood to attention with his chest stuck out, as proud as punch, and said, 'Yeah. So this is what the place looks like!'

PET

ON THAT SAME trip in 1997, one of my teammates was lucky enough to find himself in a bar talking to a stunning Penthouse Pet. He knew she was a Penthouse Pet because she told him so – and who was he to doubt her? She was absolutely gorgeous. True, she was packing more silicone than IBM, but who was worried about that? I find it amusing when women turn to men and say, 'Those are fake.' Girls, let me tell you now – we don't care.

Anyway, here was this Penthouse Pet, or so she said. (Quite frankly, I wouldn't have recognised her. On the odd occasion I read *Penthouse*, it's only for the articles.) And she was talking to my teammate. After a while an American guy sauntered over and merged in with the conversation, dropping witty repartee and coming across as quite the smoothy. Our man saw his chance slipping away, so he dug deep. Real conversation went out the window and it became a battle of one-upmanship. The stories got bigger and bigger, but each time our man thought he'd trumped his American foe, the playboy would strike back with a vengeance. Something had to be done, and done fast. My teammate was seeing bragging rights for the next five footy trips disappearing from his grasp.

Just when he thought he was about to scramble back once and for all, the playboy played his ace: he suggested that the

Pet might like to come to a club he knew around the corner, and they could leave as soon as his new Lotus Elite sports car was brought around. Our boy realised he was up against it here. He thought quickly and excused himself to go to the bathroom. Once out of sight, he sprinted to the concierge and requested the hotel limo, greasing the man's palm with his request.

While my teammate was organising the limo to be brought to the front, Lotus Playboy was talking to the bellboy and arranging for his car to be brought around, too. The damsel emerged from the hotel, expecting to be whisked away in a Lotus, to see the hotel portico blocked in by the biggest white limo she had ever seen. The Lotus was nowhere to be found – there wasn't enough room for it to get in.

Our man, cool under pressure, strode up to the Pet and said, 'Look, I thought the guy with the Lotus might turn out to be unreliable, so I had my driver bring the car up. Where can I take you?' She looked around, saw no Lotus and no Lotus driver and, shrugging, climbed into the back of the limo for a ride in luxury to the nearest nightclub. The story goes that they never made it there.

If you want to know what happened, I think it was in the 'Letters' section of the December issue: *Dear Penthouse, you'll never guess what happened to me. I was at a hotel in California when this beautiful girl spoke to me* . . .

PART 2
JOYS OF YOUTH

PRICE OF FAME

THE SUMMER of 1983–84 dragged for me. I was a 205 cm tall young man with all the coordination that comes with that. I had pimples on my face, stars in my eyes and a whole nine games of league football under my belt.

Most of the time I could walk down the street without being stared at, because as yet nobody had any idea who I was, and that suited me fine. (Don't get me wrong – there's nothing wrong with being in the public eye. I quite enjoy it, and am amazed at those famous folk who complain about how the media invade their privacy, and then two weeks later are selling their story to a magazine for six figures. Fame is fleeting, as they say, and perspective is everything.)

Getting back to that summer of 1983–84, I was enjoying just being eighteen. Like all my mates, I would queue up at the pub to get in, and just like them I would stand around for a while before sidling up to a young lady and asking for a dance. I'd be surprised when she said no despite the fact that I was wearing my best corduroy jacket, but I'd go back to the bar and let the boys know she wasn't my type. They'd all agree and then I'd try the whole procedure again. Eventually, at about midnight, we'd go to the car and head home.

As a teenager I didn't really have a lot of luck with the ladies. I remember one St Valentine's Day going out and thinking the night had gone really well. I'd paid for dinner at a lovely restaurant, bought flowers from those people who come to the table and shame men into buying flowers, and taken my date on a horse-and-carriage ride through town – but at the end of the night she just shook my hand and said, 'Next year, can you please use another escort agency?' I was devastated.

However, my fortunes were about to change. Three weeks into the 1984 season I had kicked 22 goals and was leading the league goal-kicking table. I was still 205 cm, still didn't have a licence to drive and still had to use all the charm I could muster just to get the family cat to sit on my lap, but none of that mattered now. I was a football star, and my life changed completely.

Now when I joined the queue to get into a venue, the bouncer would come down the line, grab me and take me in for free, and, more often than not, give me a drink card. Although the card was a generous gesture, I wasn't drinking alcohol due to my playing commitments. Over a night I couldn't drink much more than four Cokes – five at the most – so I was hardly costing them a fortune. I think I'm the only guy in the history of the game who never abused the drink-card privilege. It was only after a couple of months that I found out I could have actually shouted other people with my card. Bugger.

So here I was with free access to pubs and other venues, discounted clothes and free drinks. I was everybody's mate, but what was of most importance to me was that girls were starting to talk to me. Gone were the days when I would come home from school crying and Mum would reassure me by saying, 'Don't worry, Paul. The reason the girls throw things at you is because they like you. They're just too embarrassed to admit it.' Now Mum was in charge of taking messages when I wasn't home and passing them on. I'd known the day

Price of fame

would come when the girls would be able to see past the gangly awkwardness of youth and access the real me, deep inside that 205 cm body, and finally they had. It was just a coincidence that it was at exactly the same time as I became relatively famous.

I didn't actually care *why* they were finally talking to me: I was just rapt they were. The challenge then became to distinguish between those girls who were staring out of genuine interest, and those who were weirdly fascinated by the tall freak-show at the bar. It became a totally unreal world and in all honesty I had a lot of trouble coping with it initially. Most teenagers aren't that confident outside their own environment, and for me, even walking down the street became a problem. Total strangers would come up to chat, which freaked me a bit and became a double-edged sword. If I ignored them I was 'that uppity bastard Paul Salmon', but if I spoke to them in my nervous state they would go away and tell their friends what a dickhead I was. I couldn't win either way.

One thing about being famous is that everyone knows you, and they're happy to tell other people they know you. For example, I went to a nightclub one evening and the bouncer saw me and brought me up to the door. 'How are you, Paul?' he said.

'Good, thanks.'
'Staying long?'
'I'm not sure. I'll see how it goes.'
'Your brother and cousins are already inside.'
'Sorry?'
'Your brother and cousins are already inside. Have a good night.'

I wandered in, looking forward to catching up with my brother, who, when I had last spoken to him an hour earlier, was in Perth. To this day I have no idea who my 'brother' was, but if he reads this I'd love to meet him.

Joys of youth

I wasn't the only one to experience a new-found family. My mum was standing in a queue at Eastland in Ringwood when the woman in front of her started to berate the staff for their lack of service. She told them they'd be sorry for treating her badly, because she was Paul Salmon's mum. Slightly outraged, because she would never behave like that, Mum tapped the woman on the shoulder and pointed out that *she* was in fact Paul Salmon's mother. The woman turned on Mum, calling her a liar and telling her to mind her own business and piss off. Mum wasn't sure what to do with this one, but, like most mums, she always seems to come through under pressure. She dug deep into her handbag and pulled out her purse, which she proceeded to open in front of the impostor. Out came a photo of me taken in the late 1960s in my cowboy outfit at a birthday party – not definitive proof of her claim, but obviously a favourite photo. The rather emotional impostor couldn't produce anything quite as convincing and trudged off into the whitegoods section, never to be seen again. I'm pretty sure she wouldn't be in a hurry to claim me nowadays.

It was about this time that I earned the nickname among my mates of 'Goat'. I'm sure you've seen those nature documentaries where the villagers tether a goat in the centre of the village, the lions come down to feed on the goat, and then the villagers surround the lions and pick them off one by one. Well, I was that goat. My mates realised that, as unattractive as I seemed to *them*, the girls still wanted to talk to me. They decided not to waste this talent. We'd go to a bar, they'd prop me up and wander a short distance away, and I'd order a drink and stand there. Before long a girl would come over with her friends to chat, at which point my mates would surround them and attempt to pick them off one by one. Unfortunately, while everyone else was dancing and celebrating their good fortune, I'd end up wandering home on my own.

LEGENDS

AFTER I INJURED my knee in 1984, I was invited to Tasmania by former Essendon player Robert Shaw (now Bombers assistant coach) to participate in a sportsmen's night. I was a bit flat emotionally and it seemed like it might not be a bad idea. And it quickly became a great idea when Robert told me I would be on a panel with a former teammate, Ronnie Andrews, and a cricketing legend, the just-retired Dennis Lillee.

A quiet night and a change of scenery were in order, or at least that was the plan. I was still on crutches and hadn't been out of the house much since the surgery, so I didn't expect to be doing anything more than meeting a hero and catching up with an old mate (Dennis and Ron, in that order).

I arrived at Wrest Point Casino in Hobart a little late and quickly showered and dressed in time for the show downstairs. It was all a bit of a rush so I didn't have time to get to know Dennis or talk to Ron before the show. I have to admit I was a tad awestruck when I was introduced to the great man, Dennis Lillee. My contribution to the panel-style show was limited, given I had only been around to accumulate stories for about as long as the red wine provided on the tables. But I had fun and played along as well as I could. Ron and Dennis carried it beautifully and I think I enjoyed it as much as the audience – probably more, as I was getting paid to sit there and soak it up.

The show finished and the three of us went to a quiet bar on the premises and made ourselves comfortable. What I didn't realise or appreciate at the time was that my two companions were seasoned campaigners and when they suggested I make myself comfortable, it was likely to be for the very long haul.

Stories flew faster than an Andrew McLeod centre-bounce clearance and I became totally engrossed – so engrossed that I took little notice of the amount we were all drinking, especially Dennis and Ron, who were going two to my one. Dennis, in particular, had me hypnotised with yarns from overseas tours, and with each story there was a specific type of drink to go with it. For example, if he was talking about being under the stars in the Caribbean with Rod Marsh, on a lounge chair near a pool, then we'd have to drink some sort of exotic cocktail that Dennis would have the bartender whip up.

Unfortunately for my constitution, but much to Ronnie's delight, Dennis had been on many tours and kept us entertained for hours. Ronnie and I were in fits of laughter as the night rolled on. It was priceless stuff and the time just seemed to flow by, along with the drinks. Dennis turned out to be a very generous man and amazing company. I had to keep pinching myself that I was there, because it hadn't been that long since I'd been one of those schoolboy fans in the outer at the MCG chanting, 'Liiiiiilleeeee, Liiiiiilleeeee!' as he came in to bowl.

Eventually the bartender called for last drinks and we accepted our fate begrudgingly before retiring to our rooms. Well, Dennis's room actually, where the party rolled on. It seemed pretty harmless – we weren't driving anywhere and certainly weren't making too much of a ruckus or disturbing anyone. The mini-bar was Dennis and Ron's last resort and I was still hanging in there, willing the night to last forever.

The clock ticked over to 5.30 a.m. and, with the mini-bar empty and a taxi booked to pick us up at 6.30 for our 7.35 flight, it appeared that the night was about to come to a close. But I was in the company of two legends of sport, both on and off the field of battle, and there was no way they were going to accept defeat. There didn't seem any point in trying to sleep when we had almost gone the full distance and none of us was getting behind a wheel.

You may be getting the impression that we were preoccupied with alcohol consumption, but you have to believe me when I tell you that the drinking was simply a by-product of an amazing chemistry on the night. In hindsight the alcohol probably wasn't necessary at all, and in part my overindulgence led me, soon after, to give up drinking until I was in my thirties, when I learned about moderation. It would be fair to say that none of us, when getting in that taxi, would have been any help to the cabbie if he'd been in need of directions.

We arrived back in Melbourne and my father was there to pick me up. Dad was rapt to meet Dennis. We said our goodbyes and Ron, who was a bit wobbly on it, asked if my old man could drop him off at work. That was no problem, so we climbed into the car. 'Where to, Ron?' asked Dad.

'The meatworks in Keilor, Alan,' Ronnie replied.

'No worries then.' And off we went.

We arrived at Ron's work and dropped him off where he asked to be left, next to a van. Dad obviously had the same question on his mind that I had on mine. 'Hey Ron, what do you do here, mate?' he asked.

'I'm a meat delivery driver, Al, and I cover the north-east of Melbourne.'

'So what are you planning on doing today?' was the obvious response from Dad.

Joys of youth

'Same ol', same ol', Al,' said Ron proudly. He pulled out the keys to the van and jumped into the driver's seat.

Now there's every chance that Ron would have done a lot of heavy breathing that day, so anyone who was delivered meat in the north-east that tasted a little like an exotic cocktail on a certain day in 1984 now knows why.

SPACE

As a player, Roger Merrett was a man's man, somebody you had to respect and look up to, or else! For over 300 games he patrolled the change rooms with the same menace he did the football field. His reputation for never taking a backward step was well earned and totally justified.

For a number of years in the early to mid-1980s, Roger was one of several mentors I had as I found my feet in league football. I often went to the more senior players for advice and revelled in their wisdom and ability to simplify the most complex of situations, with statements such as, 'It's always best not to ask the coach for anything when he's mad.' Not rocket science, you might think, but a football club demands that one so young and naive seek counsel from those who have 'smoked the pipe', so to speak. The journey through life in a clubroom is a group effort and therefore it is wise to share experiences and seek advice on all levels. Otherwise you might appear aloof or, worse still, get a reputation as a 'lone ranger' – someone who only looks out for number one, rows their own boat, is a Robinson Crusoe, a stinky boy, a know-it-all, a— I think you get my drift.

I have fond memories of my introduction to the system. As a raw seventeen-year-old, I was sometimes required to light the cigarettes of my older teammates when their hands were

Joys of youth

full with milkshakes and liquorice straps from Mrs C's milk bar across the road from Windy Hill. The senior players called this 'The Apprenticeship' and all new kids went through it. Or at least that's what they told me when they were flushing my head in the urinal.

I made my debut in 1983 and played nine games that season. Although most of my time was spent on the bench, I had the occasional run on the field. It was a tough forward line to play in, as it was dominated by some of the biggest, meanest hombres going around. The likes of Merrett, Terry Daniher (the captain) and Paul Van Der Haar roamed their space with total disregard for anyone, including a young and impressionable teammate like myself. I found it almost impossible to go for a mark without one or all of them flying over the top and attempting the mark themselves. The usual consequences were that no one would get it or someone would get hurt. Terry, in particular, had mastered the art of making the impossible pack mark even more impossible.

Kevin Sheedy, our coach, loved the idea of having a big forward line, and always encouraged us to attack the footy and go for it. In his eyes, it was a small price to pay if we sometimes all went for it together. It was frustrating at times, but as the new kid on the block it wasn't my place to do anything except play the game on their terms. And so it was that four of the biggest guys in the game did their level best to mark everything that came into the forward line, and hang the consequences.

One day, in an effort to define my place in the pecking order, I sought out Roger for some one-on-one to identify what I should do. I was over the moon when he volunteered a piece of advice that I never forgot over my own long career. When I asked him what I should do when the forward line got a little crowded, he replied, 'Tell 'em all to f--- off.'

'What – you want me to tell you, Terry and Vanda to f--- off?' I said, a little hesitantly.

Space

'Yeah,' said Rog. 'Just tell us all to f--- off out of your space so you can get a run at it.' This was enlightening stuff, and I went away feeling empowered and ready to assert myself in the heat of battle. I saw it as a green light from a senior player to step up and be counted as one of them, a ridgy-didge member of the team.

The next Saturday came around and I was excited for more reasons than just a game of football. Today was the day when I would legitimately get to tell certain club legends to 'F--- off'. I prepared with plenty of zest and my team talk before the game was inspiring, or so I thought until the boot studder told me to shut up for talking drivel. (At least, that's what I thought he said – his cleft palate made him difficult to understand.)

Not long into the first quarter the ball came forward and I could see unfolding in front of me another case of 'all in' or every man for himself. Thinking quickly, I called out to Roger, my mentor and ally in the plan, 'F--- off out of my space!' It had to work – it was his idea. 'If he goes, they'll all follow' was my theory.

At my words Roger spun around, ready, I thought, to acknowledge my new authoritative approach. Instead, he looked stunned. His eyes blazed and, with his fists clenched, he yelled, 'You'd better not be f---in' talking to me!'

Sigh. It was another example of 'Do as they do, not as they say'.

RUCKMAN

As a 205 cm tall footballer who was born to ruck but played full-forward with a modicum of success, I heard a lot of frustrating and annoying statements and questions over the years. But there was one absolute standout.

It wasn't 'What's the weather like up there?' or 'Watch your head' or 'Can you hear me up there?' It wasn't even 'How's the knee?' or 'Pull ya finger out, Salmon!' None of these got to me nearly as much as this one gem. Anyone who has followed my career over the past twenty years is probably as sick of it as I became. So here it is, the bane of my life: 'Which do you prefer, Fish – ruck or full-forward?'

In one way it was flattering to have a choice, but in another it was a question that haunted me until the day I arrived at Hawthorn Football Club in 1996 to start my career anew as a ruckman. The reason it haunted me so much was that, from the outset, I didn't really answer it honestly. Why? Because my wily old coach K. Sheedy had suggested a response that would supposedly relieve all the pressure and enable me to concentrate solely on football.

Well, that was the plan.

About five weeks into season 1984, Kevin and I were invited to a sponsor's function in Albury. At that point I had registered a little over 30 goals and was riding a wave of publicity and attention possibly unprecedented at the time. As we flew high over the Great Divide, Kev and I chatted over a drink – me over a long, cold water and Kev over a long, cold chardonnay (or three). He was always at his best and most incisive, in my opinion, with the help of a bit of Yarra Valley grape nectar.

Anyway, we were mulling over the problems of the world when the topic of how I was coping came up. Always one to take the opportunity to talk about myself, I was forthcoming with a question that was becoming a bit of a pain in the glutes. 'Sheeds,' I said, 'all the journos want to know if I would prefer to play at full-forward or in the ruck, and it's starting to annoy me a little.' Oh, the irony in that statement and the foresight exhibited by one so young.

Kev thought for a second, performed his now-customary caressing of his chin between his thumb and pointer finger and said, 'Tell 'em you're a ruckman.'

'Why?' I asked, with youthful inquisitiveness.

'Well, because it will ease the pressure on you as a full-forward and allow me to throw you into the ruck sometimes without anybody wondering what the hell I'm doing.' It sounded like a stroke of genius to me, but then again, I was under the influence of thirteen waters, so maybe I was just in a hurry to get to the men's room.

So it was that from that moment forward, whenever I was asked the dreaded question, I would answer, 'The ruck.' The monster was born.

Unfortunately the plan went a little awry, as fans thought I became preoccupied with rucking to the detriment of my performance as a full-forward, and that at times I was even unhappy with my role in the team. Nothing could have been further from the truth. There wasn't much I could do to convince people of my happiness as a goal-kicker, so I rolled with it for the next twelve years. Living a lie, there was no going back.

Joys of youth

It wasn't the last piece of advice I took from Kevin, and most of his other pearls of wisdom proved to be great. The moral of the story? Think long and hard before taking advice from a man drinking cheap chardonnay!

TRUST ME

IF YOU'RE A parent, like me, you'll be familiar with a saying parents occasionally use to help deal with the mistakes or poor decisions of our children. The old 'We were all young once' gets trotted out to assist us in coping with parenthood and to remind us that we too may have stuffed up on occasion when we were young and impulsive. I remember all too well those times when I couldn't move on quickly enough from an indiscretion and desperately hoped no one found out about it.

One of my favourite little instances of such a situation involves an old teammate of mine from the mighty Hawks. He was recruited from interstate and when he arrived in Melbourne, the club arranged for him to board with a lovely middle-aged widow who lived not far from the club. The player was young, single and, some wives and girlfriends of players suggested, quite handsome. Personally I couldn't see it – but then again I think I look all right in the morning, so who was I to say.

One weekend the widow went away with some friends, leaving our hero to his own devices at home. This was his chance for a little freedom, so he laid down some plans that included a big night on the town. He went out with a few of the boys and proceeded to have one of his best nights in a long time, knowing that if he got lucky with the ladies he'd have the whole house to himself.

This particular evening he was fortunate enough to 'score' and invited the young lady back to 'his' place for a coffee (or whatever they invite girls back for nowadays). A little soft mood music, a comfortable couch, some childhood 'I was a klutz' stories and before you know it, they were at it like it was their last act before a nuclear strike. He couldn't have planned it better – except that he had overlooked the fact that he had early-morning training the next day.

In the morning the couple awoke to the realisation that they might have to chew their respective arms off, but to their surprise it wasn't as bad as feared. He told her he had to take off for training and that it would be a couple of hours before he returned. He had no idea what her name was, nor did he bother to ask for a contact phone number. A repeat performance was not at the top of his mind at the time. So he went off to training without a second thought about the vulnerable position he was leaving the house in.

Our hero returned some three hours later to find that the girl had cleaned out everything of any value. Electricals, jewellery, clothing – you name it, she'd taken it. He was devastated. What had he done? How was he going to break the news to the woman who had taken him in and trusted him with her home for two days? It was a terrible mistake and there was nothing he could do to fix it.

On top of all this he didn't even get the chance to ask his date the question on every guy's lips after a night of passion such as the one he'd enjoyed: 'How was I?'

PART 3
MATCH-DAY MADNESS

COACH'S BOX

TO THE AVERAGE footy fan, it probably looks as if everything runs like clockwork for a football club on match days. However, I'm here to tell you that this well-oiled machine is just an illusion, especially during the pressure-cooker environment of the match itself.

Pressure brings out the best in some and the worst in others. Decisions can lack their usual clarity and even the best-laid plans can sometimes go off the rails. Memorable statements are made and regrettable actions are taken that, fortunately, usually fade with time.

Well, I did say *usually*. I've decided I should share some incidents that certain individuals would prefer never saw the light of day, and some stories that simply have to be told so they live forever as a reminder of what is so human about professional sport.

Match-day madness

THE WELL-KNOWN former coach of a northern neighbour, in a game at the Gabba, has his side down by a few points with a couple of minutes left to go in the game. A player whom he doesn't hold in particularly high regard makes a mistake deep in the forward line and gives away a silly free kick, with which the opposition rebounds out to safer territory.

The coach goes off his tree, yelling obscenities and basically losing control, while the team manager, trying to calm the situation, states that they can still win the game as there is plenty of time left.

However, the coach is at the point of no return and, without thinking, starts to land a volley of punches into the kidneys of the team manager. With the victim buckling at the knees, the assistant coach has to grab the coach and pull him away. All this while the game is still in the balance, with minutes on the clock.

A LONG-TIME SERVANT of the Hawthorn Footy Club and runner for coach Allan 'Yabby' Jeans was George Stone. Yabby was noted for his ability to get names a little confused, and George shared a couple of his favourite stories with me.

Yabby: 'Who's on Purple?' (Actually meant to say, 'Who's on Alvin?' as in Carlton's Tom Alvin.)

Yabby: 'Who's on Gas Stove?' (Actually meant to say, 'Who's on Gastev?' as in John Gastev, of Brisbane Bears fame.)

Coach's box

ALLAN 'YABBY' JEANS barks down the phone to George, 'Do you see that big blond poofter at centre half-forward?' referring to Dermott Brereton. 'Tell that poofter to take his high heels off and get a kick!'

George takes off onto the ground knowing full well that by delivering such a message he is taking his life into his hands. He arrives not far from where Dermott is standing and has a moment of inspiration when he sees Russell Morris nearby – who is also blond but less threatening than Dermott and has been playing a blinder. George yells at him, 'Russell, get your high heels off and get a kick!'

Russell looks perplexed and just shrugs his shoulders. George arrives back at the bench and the phone rings again. It's Yabby. 'How did you go?'

'Not bad,' says George. 'I think Morris will give us a lift.'

HAWTHORN ARE PLAYING the Brisbane Lions at the Gabba in the late 1990s. We are well down at half-time and sit in the rooms pondering our situation. Just about everyone in the team needs to lift their game, and we could use a miracle to get us out of this one.

A senior member of the match committee, one of the coach's right-hand men, approaches a player sitting in front of his locker with his head bowed in an apparent state of disillusionment. 'And as for you,' he says sternly, 'you have to bloody pull your finger out and get a bloody kick or you'll be in the twos for f---ing sure next week!'

Match-day madness

The player, who is dressed in his tracksuit top and bottom, looks up, puzzled, and replies, 'But I haven't been on yet.'

'Oh. Well, when you do, make sure you get a kick,' comes the hasty and embarrassed response, before the man turns and heads back to the magnetic team board to double-check it before unleashing his next barrage.

ONCE UPON A TIME players used occasionally to take a leak on the ground at quarter-time. I never really enjoyed standing over a teammate and covering for him as he knelt to piddle on the ground in front of up to 80 000 people. You could never trust his aim or timing, and your boots would often get splashed, or the huddle would disperse to expose a bloke on one knee with another standing there watching. Not sure how that might look to impressionable children.

Relieving yourself on the ground has now been outlawed, and players are savvy about having a leak before they go out. One favourite story of mine is about the urge to go – not that of a player, but of a coach. This particular former coach liked to relieve himself in the box. I guess when you gotta go, you gotta go! During the course of a game it wasn't unusual for him to request the use of a cup for purposes other than rehydrating. The occasion in question went something like this.

The coach shouts urgently, 'Get me a cup! Someone pass me a bloody cup!'

A cup is located and passed to the front of the box, where the somewhat relieved coach does just that: relieves himself.

Coach's box

A few seconds pass and everyone's attention has returned to the game, when the coach again raises his voice. Much to everyone's surprise he barks, 'Get me another cup! This one's nearly full!'

⚫

A COACH IS in the box going ballistic at his runner for answering back, but doesn't realise he has the phone upside down. His assistant chimes in with 'Hey, boss . . .'

The coach yells, 'WHAT DO YOU WANT? WHAT THE HELL DO YOU WANT?!'

'Your phone is upside down,' says the assistant bravely.

'Oh.' The coach turns the phone around. 'Can you hear me now?' he says into it. Unfortunately for the runner, it wasn't enough to stop the tirade of abuse.

⚫

VICTORIA VERSUS TASMANIA, late 1980s. The Victorian 'B' team are taking on the Taswegians at North Hobart oval, with lots of top-line players in the side, including Paul Roos, Doug Hawkins, Danny Frawley, Darren Millane and Mick Martyn, to name a few. 'The Hawk' isn't at his absolute best and the coach calls the runner and says, 'Tell Hawkins to come off.'

Dougie is known for having a passionate dislike for being dragged, no matter how badly he is travelling. The runner goes out to him, but returns quickly with no success. 'He won't come off,' is the runner's response to the coach.

'Tell him to come off now!' retorts the coach, before hastily adding, 'If he tells you to f--- off, tell Darren Williams to come off!'

NICE LITTLE STORY about Damian Drum coaching the Allies in Brisbane a few years back. The phone rings in the coach's box and Damian answers, 'Hello, Damian Drum here.'

The runner calling from the bench replies, 'I know who you are, mate.'

SHEEDS

I HAD A TEAMMATE at Essendon back in the late 1980s and early 1990s who used to rack up plenty of possessions week in, week out. He was a good bloke by the name of Gavin Keane, and he was what we call in football a 'ball magnet'. He was very good at being on the end of a lot of handballs and kicks out wide to his favourite wing at Windy Hill.

Every team needs a Gavin Keane type: one who links up well and delivers with penetration into the forward line. The only thing Gavin lacked in his game was penetration. Good sides have the right balance of ball-getters and finishers who complement one another, but Gav developed a reputation for being a little too wide when taking possession. He was in trouble if the opposition were getting more of the ball than us, because that meant he was getting less of it.

One day things aren't working as well as the team would like, and Gav isn't compiling the sorts of numbers he has become accustomed to. Sheeds is becoming increasingly frustrated and eventually has had enough. Picking up the phone in the coach's box, he calls the team runner on the bench and says, 'Tell that bloody Keane that if he enjoys calling for the ball so much from the second level of the grandstand, I'll buy him a reserved seat so he can bloody well sit there every week – because he won't be playing football for me ever again!'

Match-day madness

Just goes to show that Sheeds does have a sense of humour under pressure.

~

SITTING HIGH UP in the Southern Stand coach's box at the MCG, Sheeds yells at a team runner sitting on the bench at ground level, 'Are you there? GET BOMFORD OFF! Are you there? GET BOMFORD OFF! Anyone there? For Christ's sake, GET BOMFORD OFF!'

With Sheeds' blood pressure at boiling point, assistant coach Mark Harvey turns to him and says calmly, 'Pick up the phone, Kev.'

~

ESSENDON ARE PLAYING Sydney on a wet and miserable Saturday afternoon in 2000 at the MCG, with Sydney fielding a less-than-full-strength team against the all-conquering Bombers. Essendon leads but the Swans are making a late charge when former Bomber, now Swan, Ryan O'Connor kicks the ball out of bounds on the full. Sheeds picks up the phone and yells at the runner, 'Get O'Connor off!'

Sheeds

The football manager taps Kev on the shoulder and says, 'O'Connor plays for the Swans now, Sheeds.'

Sheeds pauses for a second before putting the phone back to his ear and saying, 'I'll get back to you.'

HORSIN' AROUND

I HAVE NEVER been a big punter. My interest in horse racing has grown only over the past few years, to the point where I now follow all the major meets around the country. It may have something to do with my role as co-host on Channel 7's *Sportsworld* on Sunday mornings, which requires me to have a strong knowledge of all sports. Whatever it is, I can tell you that I am now a 'Sport of Kings' convert and enjoy going to the races, where my punting is confined to an occasional each-way bet.

I've had many teammates over the years with a great passion for the races, including ownership of horses, a lot of form guides and lusty betting. Players like Mark Harvey, Darren Bewick and Greg Anderson at the Bombers, and John Platten, Jason Dunstall and Robert 'Dipper' DiPierdomenico of Hawthorn, are some of the keenest track watchers I have had the pleasure of witnessing lose money. I say 'pleasure' because although it pains me to see anyone lose money, those guys had plenty anyway. The thing that intrigued me the most was that no matter how much they lost, they got enormous enjoyment out of the involvement (mind you, there were many wins as well).

It's common for a race meet to coincide with a football match, which can prove to be a minor distraction for those

Horsin' around

team members with more than a passing interest in a race result. Of course, there was the recent example, in 2002, of Kevin Sheedy's champion horse and winner of a Blue Diamond, Bel Esprit, racing in a Group 1 interstate at the same time as the Bombers were playing a home-and-away game. The scoreboard showed the race in progress and for a few moments Sheeds was caught in a dilemma of what to watch. It was jokingly suggested that during the race he sent the runner out onto the field to get Bel Esprit into the action by shifting her to ruck rover! It didn't help, unfortunately, as both of Kevin's loves went down that day.

A former Bomber and Hawk teammate of mine, and a good friend, Barry Young, is a great follower of horse racing. He is an 'all or nothing' sort of guy and his passions are full-on, as evidenced by what happened at a game in the late 1980s at the MCG. Barry loves to punt and would let the world know when he had a win, but was never too forthcoming with the details of a loss. I've come to realise that this is generally the case with punting, but I think it was Barry's ability to ride a win for as long as he could that made him stand out from the pack.

I was injured one particular Saturday afternoon and in the lead-up before the game was doing the supportive and encouraging rounds of the players in the change rooms. Barry called me over to the vicinity of the 'wet area' and whispered, 'Hey, Fish.'

'What, mate?' I asked, expecting to be asked my thoughts on his opponent, or even for some tips on how to play half-back flank. I should have known better – this was Barry Young, who never sought guidance as he had all the answers already. It was one of his most endearing qualities, as a matter of fact.

'I need you to put this fifty bucks on number seven in the third at Caulfield,' he said.

Match-day madness

'What! You want me to place a bet for you?' I was genuinely taken aback – it had never occurred to me that a player might be thinking about placing a bet just before a game.

'Yeah, the TAB is up on the next level, 50 metres along. Just whack it on the nose,' were Barry's instructions.

'Whack who on the nose?' came my logical response, or so I thought.

'Place the bet for a win, you big idiot, and you'd better do it now so I know it's done before the game starts. That way I can relax and concentrate on getting a kick.'

'You can't be serious!' I said, still disbelieving.

'My oath I am! So can you move your arse?' Now I knew he meant it. After wandering around the rooms for a few minutes seeing more of the boys, I was again approached by Baz. 'Have you done it?' he wanted to know.

'Not yet.'

'Why not?'

'Because you didn't ask nicely.'

'WHAT!' Youngy rarely appreciated my sense of humour. I told him, 'Trust me – I'll get around to it.'

The game got under way and I kept a close eye on Baz. When race results were flashed up on the big screen I watched for any breaks in his concentration. Sure enough, whenever the ball was out of his range, he would glance at the scoreboard to see if his race was coming up.

The siren sounded to end the first quarter and the boys headed for the huddle. They hadn't made a great start and I could tell Sheeds was going to rip into them a bit. Out the back of the group was Baz, still keeping a close eye on the scoreboard. All of a sudden the results of his race flashed up on the screen. His horse had gone down by a short half-head (just wanted to impress you with some racing lingo) and he let out a big 'Oh s---!'

Sheeds obviously thought something serious had happened and barked, 'What's wrong?'

Quick-thinking club doctor Bruce Reid yelled, 'Nothing, Kev. Youngy just saw his stats for the first quarter!'

The race loss totally ruined Youngy's day and he went on to take out his frustration on an opponent, got reported and was subsequently suspended. But the funniest thing about the whole episode was that I had forgotten to place the bet! I don't know what I would have done if the horse had got up. Youngy never knew that the fifty bucks that went on the bar for the boys that night was his. There was only one winner out of the incident, and that person was me.

OFFICIAL
NONSENSE

A TEAM MANAGER notices a player kneeling in front of his locker before the game, saying a prayer prior to running out on the field. Not one to miss an opportunity, and being of little faith himself, he wanders over and says, 'You're going to need more than Him to get a kick today!'

BEFORE EVERY GAME of league football, the umpires enter the rooms during the warm-up to shake the players' hands, wish them luck and speak briefly with the coaches. One match day I'm kicking with some of the boys when the umpires come in. A teammate leans across and mutters, 'Watch this, Fish.'

It turns out the player has some history with a particular umpire in a business deal gone wrong, and wants to spook him a bit. He kicks the ball a little harder and a little flatter towards the umpire, meaning to hit the wall next to him and give him a fright. Unfortunately it all goes horribly wrong and we

Official nonsense

watch as the ball sails towards the unsuspecting umpire's head. It connects with a thud and sends him reeling back against the wall and onto his knees. We're stunned and the player concerned looks on in total disbelief.

Trainers rush from everywhere to the umpire's aid, picking him up and placing him on a rubdown bench. He is dazed but not hurt and is able to stagger around the group to finish formalities. When he gets to the offending player, it all becomes clear to him and he realises it may not have been an accident. With a knowing look, he nods to the player and says, 'I'm going to enjoy umpiring today.'

EVERY LEAGUE CLUB has a computer and video analyst who puts a lot of time into preparing game tapes and highlight tapes for the coaches and players. There's also the occasional motivational tape requested by the coach for use just prior to taking the field, to put the finishing touches to the players' preparation.

Ken Judge teed up one of these with Hawthorn's video man, Phil, for a game against Geelong a few years back. We arrive in the coach's room to find the video and TV set up ready to go and Ken standing near the whiteboard waiting with great anticipation to give a pre-match address to remember. According to the plan, all Ken has to do to show the tape is press 'Play' on the VCR at the appropriate moment.

The coach has brought us to an emotional peak when he decides it's time for the video package. He walks over to the

Match-day madness

VCR and pushes the button – well, *a* button, at least – and it all goes pear-shaped. The TV crackles and snows and does everything but show the motivational collection Phil has put most of his week into.

Ken is obviously to blame for the problem, but he's not about to admit it. Phil stands there, his face growing longer by the second, like a man awaiting the executioner's axe. Finally it comes, the moment we've all been expecting but nonetheless dreading. 'F--- ya, Phil!' shouts Ken. 'Can't you do anything right?' He's looking for the nearest item to use as a projectile when a quick-thinking assistant coach yells, 'All right, boys, let's go and get into 'em!'

Poor Phil. It's a stay of execution, so to speak. He knows it's not the last he'll hear about it, but for the next two hours he can at least make a phone call and order his last meal.

IN THE MOOD

HAVING MUSIC PLAYING during the team warm-up is not uncommon in football, and being the old groover that I am, I used to enjoy kicking the ball around with a teammate and maybe cutting a few moves to the beat. The selection of what music to play was often left up to whichever player had the largest CD collection, which supposedly meant we could assume he had good taste. Wrong! Sometimes we got served up some real trash, even allowing for the fact that musical tastes vary from person to person.

So I'm kicking around with Mark 'Heebie' Graham at Subiaco when Hawthorn is over there to play the West Coast Eagles in the late 1990s. We're listening to some absolute rubbish that has been provided by team psychologist Anthony Clarica. Now it must be understood that as a conveyer of motivational music, Clari makes a great psych. After moonwalking to Michael Jackson's 'Bad', Heebie and I are eagerly awaiting the next track and thoroughly enjoying being totally relaxed before the game. On it comes: the theme to TV's *The Lone Ranger*, which, for those of you too young to remember, is the famous *William Tell Overture* by Rossini.

We can't believe what we're hearing and break up laughing. I mean, I like being relaxed before a game and having a late build-up of intensity closer to the official warm-up, but the

Match-day madness

Lone Ranger theme is taking it too far. I know this is hard to believe an hour before a game, but we totally lose it. We're in hysterics, tears running down our faces and doubled over with laughter. Teammates walk past shaking their heads as Heebie and I mimic riding imaginary horses around the room, all the while keeping the footy active. Clari stands there in disbelief at the fact that his carefully chosen compilation is having a very different effect to the one he intended. More players join in and it's close to getting out of control. The coaches are in a meeting, so this behaviour is allowed to go on for several minutes. We're lucky Ken Judge can't see what's happening outside his door.

Eventually things settle down. We go on to win the game and, naturally enough, the *Lone Ranger* theme becomes an anthem of sorts for a short time. Whenever Heebie and I need a reminder that football isn't always such a serious business, we have a listen to it.

(Anthony Clarica is now the fitness adviser and psych for AFL umpires. No wonder they look so at ease before games!)

THINGS WILL NEVER again be quite the way they were in the days when league football was played on suburban grounds and vices like drinking and smoking were looked upon as necessary evils of a player's preparation and recovery. A midweek drink or a donut before a game were never going to kill you, and a fag at half-time was seen simply as a nerve settler. Not that I ever smoked, but I had plenty of teammates who did. It was all a far cry from the strict fitness regimes of today's supreme athletes.

I remember a game at Windy Hill when we gathered for the half-time address in the rooms and nobody even bothered with a head count, as it was assumed that no player would risk missing a Kevin Sheedy verbal spray. No player knowingly, that is. When Kevin had finished purging himself of his demons we were sent back out to lift the tempo in the second half. We took up our positions and it became apparent that we were missing someone. Yes, we had left one behind in the rooms. He was in the sauna, chugging on a gasper!

A PLAYER ARRIVES at Waverley Park without an official pass and asks the gate attendant if he wouldn't mind letting it slide. The gate attendant replies that there is a crackdown on players not having entry passes and he's not allowed to.

The player tries to explain that the team will be in trouble if he can't take his place on the field. The gate attendant sees his opening and chimes in with, 'Mate, the way you've been playing, I'll just give my grandma a ring and she can fill in for you.'

If there hadn't been a few thousand witnesses present, the gate attendant might have needed a visit from his grandma – in hospital!

Match-day madness

IT'S HALF-TIME at the MCG and the Bombers make their way into the rooms. Aboriginal superstar Michael Long is looking a little proppy and the doctor rushes over to look into the problem. 'You all right, Mick?'

'Yeah,' says Mick, 'copped a knock on the thigh. Just a bit of a corky, I think.'

'Give us a look,' says the doc. 'Where is it? Might be able to see some bruising.'

Quick as lightning, Longy says, 'You think you're so good – you find it!'

A COUPLE OF the boys are driving down the highway to play Geelong at Kardinia Park. Running a bit late, they may be exceeding the speed limit a little and consequently get pulled over by our friends in the police force. It's the usual drill, with the Sarge asking why they're speeding. The wittier one, in the passenger seat, reaches into his bag of silly things to say to policemen and explains, 'We're running a little late on our way to kick some Cat arse!'

The policeman pauses for a second, then says, 'That might've been the case before you got pulled over by a Geelong supporter. Time for a roadworthy, mate.'

In the mood

Apparently the looks on their faces are worth the price of the fine, because the good-humoured copper sends them on their way, confident the car's occupants won't prove to be too big a handful for his beloved Cats.

THIRD QUARTER OF a game at Windy Hill. The runner races out to a player on the half-forward flank and says, 'The coach wants to pull you off!'

'Surely that can wait till three-quarter time, can't it?' comes the quick reply.

SIR ROBERT MENZIES, then prime minister of Australia, was visiting the Essendon change rooms after a particularly tough Bombers win and struck up a conversation with the club doctor of the day.

As they got more comfortable with one another, and players were making their way to the shower, the doctor let slip which player had the biggest penis (as you do). This seemed to be of particular interest to the nation's leader, and he requested the company of said player. Our rather chuffed hero enthusiastically bounded up to meet the special guest, unaware of the information that had been shared. They were introduced and before long the PM said, 'Apparently you and I have something in common.'

'What's that?' asked the intrigued footballer.

'I do believe that in this room we have two of the biggest pricks in Australia!'

DICE OF LIFE

NOT REALLY A 'match day' story, but a good follow-up!

In a league football club, one of the most dreaded consequences of a big loss is the 'curfew'. It's probably less common now than it used to be, but can still be used to great effect by the coach, as it robs the boys of their chance to shed the stresses of the week and drown the misery of a bad or unexpected loss.

When I was playing, there was always someone who broke the curfew – those guys who rolled the dice of life and hoped they wouldn't be found out. Getting caught breaking a curfew could have dire consequences and put you off side with the coach forever. A high price to pay for a night of rebellion, some might suggest. But the rule does have a point: *Cop it on the chin and pull your finger out on the track. Play well and there'll be no more curfews.*

If the coach got wind of a possible breach, it was always advisable for the offending party to get straight onto the front foot and confront the coach to avoid a humiliating dressing-down in front of teammates.

But there were times when the coach was simply too good, when he'd be one step ahead and ready to pounce so he could demonstrate his power and authority. One such occasion, when a player didn't see it coming, was when I was playing for

Match-day madness

Hawthorn. We were being punished for a poor showing in Perth and Ken Judge imposed a curfew on us: *Home straight away. Do not pass go, do not go to the nearest ATM.* It was fine by me, as it was the usual drill for those of us who were committed family men (or, in my case, knackered old men). Some of the other guys grumbled, but that was understandable, and a relatively normal reaction.

When I arrived for training on the Monday I heard that one of the boys – let's call him 'Huggy' – had seen fit to bend the rules. 'Gutsy,' I thought, given the risks attached. Word quickly got around as to who it was and we knew that the match review might be messy. It started normally, with Ken addressing the ordinary manner in which we had played and telling us it wasn't acceptable. Fair enough, but then he uttered nine words I won't forget in a hurry. 'Something else is not acceptable,' he barked. 'Anyone break the curfew?'

No hands went up and I instinctively cringed. Ken knew something, and it would be in the best interests of the perpetrator to come clean.

'Anyone?' Ken said, in a more threatening tone. Again no one responded, and my head dropped into my hands as I saw what was coming. 'What about you, Huggy? Did you go out?'

'No,' said Huggy, a little unconvincingly.

'Huggy, did you go out?' Ken persisted.

'No,' came the reply. This was going to get ugly if Huggy didn't admit the error of his ways, and quick.

'Huggy,' said Ken, 'did you go out? This is your last chance.'

'Yeah,' admitted a crestfallen Huggy. 'I went to the Geebung hotel for one drink.'

'You are dumb, Huggy!' yelled Ken. 'Did you go anywhere else?'

'No.'

'Did you?'

'No.'

Dice of life

'Last chance!'

'Okay, I popped into the Star Bar for a minute,' said a shattered Huggy.

'You are possibly the dumbest bloke I've ever met!' screamed Ken. 'Anywhere else?'

'No.'

'Huggy!'

'Okay, okay, I put my head around the corner at the Motel, but I didn't go in.'

If it hadn't been so serious I would have been on the floor in fits of laughter at this exchange, but the coach was not in a forgiving mood. Huggy went on to deny attending another two bars before admitting he'd ended up leaving the Tunnel at 7 a.m., thus breaking the curfew non-compliance record by a staggering four hours. Some of the boys probably wanted to hoist him onto their shoulders and organise a street parade, but it wasn't the time for that.

By now Ken's blood pressure was through the roof, and the room was deathly silent. Huggy got the biggest dressing-down of all time and all we could do was watch. Any shred of dignity or self-respect he had left was squeezed out like an orange in a juicer. He had rolled that dice of life with conviction, but had made the big mistake of thinking that the more bars he went to, the longer the odds of his getting caught.

In some eyes Huggy went up a notch that fateful Monday afternoon, but to most of us he was just another victim of the system – a system that has eyes everywhere and voices only too willing to speak, belonging to people who then sit back and enjoy watching their victim's life take a turn for the worse.

Was Huggy wrong? Yes.

Was he dumb? More naive than dumb.

Is he a hero? Only to those who see the system as something to be bucked.

Did he have a long career at Hawthorn? No.

PART 4
MATES
RATES

FOLLOW YOUR DREAM

FOOTBALL CLUBS ARE chock-full of characters, none more colourful than the dozens of players who grace the change rooms during your playing career. From conservative to complex, cool to just plain mad, you learn to accept them for who they are and what they have to offer the team. After all, it's whether they can help you win a premiership that counts, not whether you're best mates.

It doesn't matter what sort of player you are: everyone has their own dreams and aspirations away from the game. Jobs, businesses, courses and investments: you name it, a footballer has tried it. We are exposed to so much opportunity, and so many people who want to help – as well as a minority of people that don't have our best interests at heart.

Athletes of all descriptions enjoy the risk element of competition. Putting it out there and seeing what comes back is half the fun. This attitude transcends the game and often means players try things that, in hindsight, they should never have attempted. Unfortunately for selected players, I remember some beauties and I just have to share them with you – because, in my opinion, it's gems like these that help make team sport so unforgettable. Better to have tried and failed than never to have tried at all!

Mates rates

IN THE LATE 1990s Ben Dixon and Justin Crawford opened a gardening business called Hawks Home Maintenance, to service Hawthorn staff and members. It would have been a great venture if they'd had any idea of what they were doing.

I think I was the first sucker to cut them a break when I invited them over to tidy up some rubbish and resurface a garden path. (I would have done it myself if my back hadn't been playing up, of course.) Mates rates and a half-decent job were all I wanted, but I should have known I was asking too much. You couldn't meet two better blokes than Ben and Justin, or, unfortunately for Jo and me, two hungrier ones. They attacked our pantry like locusts through a wheat field and left us nothing but crumbs for dinner. If we'd deducted from the bill the value of what they ate, they would have owed us!

The job they ended up completing for us was pretty good, in fact, although I've since learned that Lilydale topping doesn't make good mulch, and that you should never hand over the keys of your beloved ride-on mower to a man wanting to use said mower to nick up to the shops for lunch.

I recommended Ben and Justin to the CEO of Hawthorn at the time, Michael Brown. It wasn't that I wanted to set him up: I honestly thought the boys had learned a lot from their experience at the Salmons. I was wrong.

The job at the Browns was to fell a tree in the front yard: not overly difficult, but still a challenge for two willing but novice gardeners. Everything went according to plan until Ben noticed that Justin hadn't properly secured a rather large branch. It was too late, and Ben could only yell, 'Let's get outta here!' as the branch fell in the direction of the house, taking out the guttering not only of the Browns' house but of their neighbours' as well. The boys watched in amazement. How could this be happening to them? And of all the houses they could have been at, this was the CEO's, the guy who does the contracts!

Follow your dream

But it didn't finish there. The branch still had to find its way to earth. Ben and Justin sat in the tree with their mouths wide open as the branch completed its journey, landing on the Browns' pride and joy: their car. They couldn't do much about the car but the boys' quick thinking saved them from the damage bill for the gutters – they hastily tied them up with some old rope from the ute and got out of there.

Life span of the business? Six months.

LONG BEFORE IT became fashionable for footballers to own cafes and bars, a couple of business-savvy footballers from Geelong started carving their way into food-and-beverage folklore. Billy Brownless and Barry Stoneham opened a small cafe in Cat-mad country, justifiably thinking that patrons would come from all over the western district for a cuppa with Bazza and Billy. They weren't far wrong, either, as the business started well.

The boys did their best to cater for the growth by working smarter rather than harder. Billy assumed responsibility for milkshakes and Bazza for sandwiches. Occasionally the two would cross over, but more often than not the plan worked like a dream.

Billy was known to make what he called 'the best shakes in the southern hemisphere', but unfortunately he had a bad habit of not handing an order over until he had ducked down behind the counter, out of sight of the public, and sampled his wares. With a huge suck he would deposit half the milkshake

Mates rates

into his own gullet, then deliver it to the paying customer half full. 'Quality, not quantity' was his motto.

One day business was steaming along when a woman approached the counter with her plate in her hand. 'Everything all right?' asked Billy.

'Would you mind taking a look at my toasted cheese sandwich, please?' the customer asked politely.

'Looks pretty damn good to me,' said Billy, glancing at it.

'Please take a closer look, would you?' came the response. With that, Billy peeled back the top slice of toast to see what the problem was. A big grin came over his face as he realised what had happened: someone had forgotten to remove the plastic wrapping from the cheese slice.

'Don't worry, love – it should still taste all right,' said a more than hopeful Billy.

'I'd like another one, if you wouldn't mind, this time preferably with no plastic,' replied the customer patiently.

Business life span? One month.

BOMBER CHAMPION MARK Mercuri hit upon a business idea in the mid-1990s that, in hindsight, he might admit wasn't really thought through well enough. The idea was to go into the fruit-merchant business with a friend at the Footscray markets. Now this kind of activity requires some pretty ugly hours, especially if you're unaccustomed to early starts – very early starts.

Mercs has never been an early riser. I remember training camps when the instructor would have to yell in his ear to

Follow your dream

rouse him. Even then he would just roll over and try to go back to sleep. He much preferred a cuddle and kiss to start the day, but the instructors were never up for it. We always had suspicions that Mercs was dreaming of being approached for the next *Men for All Seasons* calendar shoot. Striking poses for the camera in your sleep is bloody hard work, apparently.

There was nothing wrong with a late finish for our party animal and chick-magnet man of the moment, but an early start? What was he thinking? Part of the deal for the new venture into fruit sales was that he had to be at the market by 4.30 every morning to do his share.

Looked okay on paper, but it was too hard in reality. Our boy never got in before 8.30, and even then he would arrive yawning and staggering about.

Business life span? One week.

A MAN I RATE in the top ten best I played with in my career is Merv Neagle. I rate Merv highly for a number of reasons, not the least of which is that he was the centreman with the most physical presence, and simply a great ball winner and finisher. In the early 1980s Merv hit upon an idea that he was confident would take him all the way to the very top of the heap when it came to small business initiatives: a mowing round.

In those days of VFL football we trained after hours so players could pursue careers or studies without needing to worry that training would get in the way. This meant there was a lot of time to kill if you didn't have an interest outside

Mates rates

football, which left some guys with way too much time to think – a dangerous pastime for a footballer, I can assure you.

Merv was as keen as mustard and went out and bought everything he needed to be the best lawnmowing man he could be: brand-new trailer, mower, blower, edger, rake, shovel, mulcher and 2-metre extendable ladder. Don't quite know where the ladder came into it, but there was no doubt Merv was ready for business. He arrived home from the shops that afternoon as proud as punch, only to find the trailer wouldn't fit in his driveway. Left with no alternative, he backed it on to the nature strip and later spent a few quiet moments with his pride and joy before retiring for the night.

Merv slept well, dreaming of neatly trimmed lawns and nicely pruned shrubs. Maybe he even contemplated some expansion issues, as the future looked bright. He awoke in the morning with a renewed spring in his step and bounded outside to say a big 'Good morning' to his new baby on the nature strip. It seems the only thing he'd forgotten to buy was a 'Take Me' sign. Come to think of it, the sign wasn't really necessary. Someone had used their initiative – that's right, it was GONE! Stolen and never to be recovered.

It was heart-breaking for Merv and enough to shatter his dream of becoming what Jim's Mowing is today. Last we heard of Merv, he was spending Sunday afternoons scouting the neighbourhood looking for his gear, suspicious of every manicured garden in the district.

I'll tell you one thing, though. Whoever took it is lucky Merv never caught up with them. It's apparently very hard trying to mow on crutches when your nose is so big you can't see where you're going.

Follow your dream

THE LONGEST RUN-UP when kicking for goal I ever saw (apart from yours truly) belonged to Michael Symons of Essendon. There's nothing wrong with a long run-up, but when it means leaving the ground to make use of the players' race, that's taking it too far, in my opinion.

One day Mick, obviously bored out of his brain, struck upon the inspirational idea of opening up Bomber Mowing (yes, more mowing rounds). It occurred to him that there must be supporters out there wanting to see a well-built young man with his top off mowing their lawn. He was right, but I think he was unaware that he wasn't the first to have the idea. However, Mick was determined to do something constructive with his spare time that didn't involve a magazine and a box of tissues, so we encouraged rather than discouraged him.

He had some work lined up if he could just get this baby on the road, so off he went to the club to ask for an advance on his contract. He outlined his plans and the fact that he already had business booked, and the club supported his enthusiasm and agreed to help get him up and running. With the money in his pocket he was off, spending up on all the latest and greatest equipment for lawnmowing and garden maintenance, just like Merv had before him. No expense was spared and it wasn't long before he looked a million bucks in gleaming new everything, from overalls to trailer stalls.

Mick signed up his first client almost immediately. It was a major corporate client who would supply regular business, which Mick would be able to use as a foundation for growth. He was on his way, with the world his grass-clipping oyster.

Did a great job on that first contract, by all reports, but it was unfortunately the last contract, as Mick pulled up stumps and decided he would rather not get his new gear too dirty. He ended up selling it a couple of years later for a fraction of the purchase price.

You simply can't put a value on a dream.

ONLY T.D.

THE FOUR DANIHER brothers, who hail from the small farming community of Ungarie in the Riverina in New South Wales, played around 800 games between them for the mighty Bombers. Terry is now the current assistant coach of Collingwood, Neale is the coach of Melbourne, Anthony runs the family business and Chris coaches somewhere up near the farm.

Bomber fans will long remember the day when all four brothers played in the same team, in Round 22 against St Kilda back in the early 1990s, down at Moorabbin. A great family, and the best teammates a bloke could hope for. Terry and Neale were both captains of Essendon, which further underlines the standing in which the family is held at Windy Hill.

Together the Daniher boys started a business specialising in window cleaning, but willing to tackle just about anything thrown their way. They loved a hard day's work and thrived on the long hours, combining them with the demands of their professional football careers. As Terry would often say, 'A bit of hard work never killed a bloke.'

One of their bigger jobs was to run a duster over the stately home of Richard Pratt. Richard is the chairman of Visy Industries and his home, 'Raheen', in the heart of the leafy

Only T.D.

eastern suburb of Kew, is well known for its size and magnificent gardens. Terry and the boys decided to kill two birds with one stone on this particular assignment, as a former club doctor lived next door and was also on the Daniher Cleaning Services books.

Terry was in the doctor's house doing what he does best (no, not drinking – cleaning) and the rest of the team were at Raheen. It was a big job and one of the things they were asked to do was clean the huge chandelier at the top of a stairway leading up to the bedrooms. The boys' task was simple enough – dust the cobwebs and change the light globes – but they weren't expecting what was to come, that's for sure.

The only access to the chandelier was halfway up the staircase, but it turned there and made it difficult to reach the chandelier. To do their job and gain access to all points, they had to spin the beautiful 18th-century light fitting. Unbeknownst to them, by doing this they were unscrewing it.

Soon Terry, working quietly next door, heard a shout: 'T.D., come quick!'

He raced in to Raheen to find three blokes, including Chris, hanging precariously from the chandelier and trying valiantly to prevent it plummeting to earth. 'Jeez!' Terry shouted. 'Hang on!'

'What choice do we have?' came the obvious reply. The quick-thinking T.D. recognised immediately that there was only one thing standing between their working for the rest of their lives to pay the damages bill and satisfying another happy customer: it all depended on how quickly he could get to the roof and remove enough tiles to grab the chandelier's suspender cable. He was up there in a flash and before the others knew it, he was looking at them from a hole in the roof and saving the day. Slowly they managed to screw the chandelier back into place and their collective sigh of relief was heard as far away as Kilmore.

However, the job wasn't done yet. The small group of mostly Italian staff who had gathered to look on were in a state of panic and, according to the boys, perilously close to needing medical attention for heart seizures. Again it was Terry to the rescue, suggesting a course of action that has calmed generations of farmers in times of emergency: 'What say I put the billy on, hey?'

As always, a cup of tea did the trick, though it was agreed by all that they'd had enough excitement in that one day to last them a century of footy seasons.

Business life span? Still going strong.

BIG BREAK

COTERIE SUPPORTERS OF football clubs are, in the main, made up of successful men and women who love their footy team and the players so much that they choose the coterie as the best means of getting as close as possible. A number of them own their own companies and as such are a valuable resource for clubs trying to find employment for players.

Something that occasionally results in frustration for both club and employer is some players' total disregard for anything that requires them to think beyond lunchtime. The players? Well, the sun will always come up tomorrow and besides, they're going to play football forever, so it isn't really a big deal.

A teammate of mine in the late 1980s was a very talented recruit from Tasmania named Bradley Plain. Now Plainy wasn't the sort of bloke to let anything worry him too much, and he had an uncanny ability to allow anything that required a decision to slide right on by. 'Why complicate a perfectly good day with an opinion or a choice?' could easily have been his motto.

He landed a job with Ron, one of Essendon's more popular coterie members, who owned a large cleaning and maintenance firm. Ron was a big bloke with a big heart who loved the company of the boys, particularly at the bar. The job represented a big break for Brad, as offers weren't exactly streaming in at the time. He arrived on his first day at work to find that Ron had gone to a lot of trouble and expense to deck his new employee out with all the equipment he would need to perform his job like a true professional: buckets, mops, squeegees, ladder, chamois and everything else he could possibly want. Brad was ready to go.

His first job was at an office block in the city, so off he trundled to start the first day of the rest of his life. For a couple of days things appeared to be going quite nicely and Plainy seemed to be coping well with the intensity of long breakfasts, brunches, lunches and smokos. It wasn't until day three that it became apparent that, for Brad, all was not well in the world of window cleaning. Ron received a call from a concerned client inquiring as to the whereabouts of the guy who was meant to be cleaning his windows. Naturally Ron thought this a little strange, as he hadn't heard from Brad. He was quick to look into it, but with no success. Brad was missing in action.

A couple more days passed and Ron couldn't locate our window cleaner with stars in his eyes anywhere. Consequently, he became concerned for Brad's welfare. Calls to the club turned up nothing and it was as if Plainy had disappeared into thin air.

It was by mere chance that four days after Brad had walked off the job without telling a soul, Ron found him sitting at the bar at the Windy Hill Social Club. 'Where have you been?' asked Ron.

'I've been meaning to call you, Ron, but haven't had a chance,' Plainy said quickly.

'What the f--- is going on?' was the obvious question from his employer.

'I just don't think I'm cut out for window cleaning, mate,' Plainy explained.

Big break

'Well, you could have had the decency to tell me, Brad,' said a very understanding and forgiving Ron. 'Look, just give me all the gear back and we'll do our best to forget about it.'

'Gear?' Plainy asked, a little coyly.

'Yeah, all the equipment I set you up with. I'd like it back.'

'Oh, but I didn't think you'd want all that stuff,' Brad said, shrinking back on his bar stool.

'So where is it?' Ron asked.

'I sold it, mate.'

Extraordinary, but true.

Job life span? Two days.

ON THE NOSE

MICHAEL LONG IS an absolute favourite of the Bomber faithful and of every player who has had the good fortune to call themselves his teammate. He is without any shadow of a doubt the most uncanny and electric footballer I've seen, as well as the best Aboriginal player. He could do things with a football that David Copperfield, the world-famous magician, couldn't do with his hat! Longy made Fred Astaire look like an amateur, the way he danced through traffic on the football field. His finals series in 1993, which took Essendon to the premiership and culminated in the Norm Smith Medal for best player in the Grand Final, was a sight to behold and no supporter or teammate will forget it.

But Longy was human – off the field, at least. All footballers at one time or another are romanced by strangers offering them the 'next big thing' in business or a 'once in a lifetime' opportunity. Often the player knows the person, while sometimes they appear from the mist and latch on like a friend from way back. For the small asking price of your credibility and a large chunk of your hard-earned, they will provide you with visions of early retirement and long days soaking up the sun on the beach adjacent to your penthouse suite, with an Audi parked in the garage. And more often than not, that's all they are and ever will be: visions.

On the nose

Longy had one of the better opportunities come his way that I ever heard of. A friend of his had got wind (you'll pardon the pun, I hope) that the local council was looking to subcontract the emptying of sewerage pits that overflow, particularly in storms. According to this guy, it was a goldmine awaiting any savvy investor willing to get their hands a little dirty – or in this case, smelly. It was a compelling offer put forward by an individual who saw Longy as his ticket out of the crappy (sorry, another one) existence he led. All Longy had to do was buy the truck and they'd be up and running. Of course, the purchase of the truck represented the major element of exposure in this initiative and all the partner was exposing was his right hand, reaching over to accept the cheque.

However, Longy saw the potential in the deal and went down to the football club to meet with the general manager of the time. He explained the opportunity and said that he just needed a significant advance on his contract to finance the purchase of the truck. The GM said that Mick and his partner would need to prepare a business plan to support their intentions before the club could provide him with the advance – a reasonable proposition on the club's behalf, as it had Longy's best interests at heart.

I'm of the opinion that when Longy told this to his friend with all the great ideas, the friend went a little pale as he realised he didn't really know what a business plan was. But he told Mick not to worry and said he would take care of it.

Two weeks later, a document envelope appeared on the desk of the general manager. Legend has it that it contained a drawing of a truck coloured in to look like a Mr Whippy van (sorry!) and with a hose out the back leading to a sewer. (It was obviously a sewer, because it had 'sooar' written on it.)

Fortunately for Longy, this one didn't see daylight. As he was later heard to admit, something just didn't smell right!

GOTTA GO!

A FORMER TEAMMATE from the mid-1980s, who will have to remain nameless, decided to start his very own fencing company. He was useful with his hands and felt he could use them for good, not evil, for a change.

His very first job was for an old lady who just loved the Bombers, and in particular our hero. She was a lovely old chook who went to every game and worshipped the ground he walked on. The fence around her house was very old and in desperate need of replacement, so she thought all her Christmases had come at once when she heard that her idol had gone into the fencing game. One phone call later and he was over there, as keen as mustard, to get stuck into his first official contract. He ripped into it with plenty of gusto, too, tearing down the fences on all sides in a matter of hours.

It wasn't long before the property resembled a scene from *Saving Private Ryan*, particularly the final scene when the soldiers are holed up in the heavily bombed town. The old lady was most impressed with his progress, and so taken by having this big hunk of man in her backyard, I understand, that she couldn't resist watching his every move.

It got to the point where, according to our well-meaning hero, it was time to go and purchase materials for the new fence. He approached the old lady seeking the necessary funds

Gotta go!

and she was only too happy to oblige and sent him on his way with a big fat cheque. The next day all the material was delivered and she couldn't believe how smoothly everything was going.

Soon after the delivery, our man arrived on the job and commenced another honest day's work. He had erected a small section of the new fence when his mobile phone rang with an offer of another job. This one was much more lucrative than the current one, but the catch was that he would have to start immediately.

It was apparently an offer too good to refuse no matter what the consequences, so he downed tools, packed up his gear and decided he could use most of the materials the timber yard had delivered for the other job. So he packed them up as well and took off, without telling the old lady and leaving the mess he had made lying all over the place.

Now I'm sure you'll agree this is very bad business practice. Surely he would come to his senses and return and finish what he started? But no, he never returned, and he's had to live with his actions ever since. Not that I think he lost too much sleep over the incident. You'll be pleased to know that his life as a fencing contractor was very brief – something about unreliability and lack of ethics, we think.

The player was reprimanded, the club assisted in the clean-up of the property and in sweeping the incident under the carpet, and everyone moved on. It was going to take a lot more than a few demolished fences to stop the old lady from cheering her idol on from the outer – despite everything, she still thought he was pretty special. Love is blind, hey!

PART 5
UNSUNG HEROES

BOMBER BACKBONE

THE PUBLIC FACE of a football club is its players, and occasionally the president as well. Everybody at the club, though, has an important part to play and most of them go unrecognised. I thought I'd dedicate a few chapters in this book to those unsung heroes, to show that their hard work is appreciated. In the main, these people are volunteers who live for the club and their roles in it on a weekly basis. As a player I often wondered to myself what they would do without their volunteer work, but I wondered even more often what *I* would do without *them*.

First up is John 'Killer' Kilby, former head trainer for the Bombers and now the footy-trip chaperone. He is one of the reasons Essendon is the club it is today, and has one eye black and the other red, loyal and passionate. John will do anything for the players and the club. He tells the worst jokes and has the loudest laugh. To cap it off, he is perhaps the only person I know who still wears a safari suit.

Then there's Bobby, the world's most effective doorman. Bobby's job is to make sure that only the people entitled to go into the dressing room get in. By 'entitled', I don't mean by appearance, I mean by having the correct pass. Bobby has been known to stop AFL supremos because they don't have the right pass. If the Australian government is serious about

Unsung heroes

keeping illegal immigrants out of the Top End, they should just station Bobby in Darwin. Nothing and no one will get through, I can promise you that.

Charlie, Kenny and Lenny are three of the trainers. As subtle and secure as their fingers are at the club, they are in many pies outside it. If you want anything, they'll just nod and say, 'Leave it to me.' You ask no questions and you're told no lies.

While Charlie, Kenny and Lenny are procuring things, Rob, Ray and Gaz do Melbourne's best rubdowns. They're gentle but firm, and if they had ever bothered to kiss me afterwards it would have been a marriage made in heaven.

There's old Jack the trainer, who taped Dick Reynolds' ankles back in the 1930s – actually it only seems like that because he's been around for so long. Jack taped me up when I was playing in the Under 19s and loves to reminisce about the old days. That would be okay occasionally, but unfortunately it's every time I bump into him. (Lucky we're mates, Jack!) You learned quickly to laugh at Jack's jokes, too, because next time he'd make sure a few leg hairs got caught under the tape, and that's not pleasant. I will never, ever say to Jo that waxing her legs can't possibly hurt.

And there's a dedicated group of ladies and one guy who, for as long as I can remember, have been whipping up soup and rolls for the boys to have after training. The soup is usually hot, delicious and served with a smile whatever the weather. I say 'usually' because of what is now called the 'Caddyshack incident', named after the scene in the film *Caddyshack* when a chocolate bar is seen floating in a pool among hundreds of swimmers, and is mistaken for something nasty.

Someone – nobody is sure who – placed a Polly Waffle in the soup during training. The ladies returned and started to stir the soup before serving it, and the Polly Waffle rose to the top. It was looking a little worse for wear due to the heat, but unfortunately that just made it more realistic. The ladies were aghast at this wanton display of gastronomic vandalism and fished the offending article out before throwing the soup away. Turns out they hadn't actually seen *Caddyshack* and didn't know someone was only joking. It was weeks before we could convince them it wasn't real – they were long, cold weeks too. Cup-A-Soup just doesn't cut it.

BRUCE 'REIDY' REID and Ian 'Rubber' Reynolds are two blokes masquerading as doctors at Essendon. I only hope they're more understanding with the patients they meet in their practice than they are when they treat players. Don't get me wrong – their medical knowledge and ability are second to none, but there's no way you can pull a sickie. If you want to avoid training, you have to have a very good reason.

For example, Scott Lucas and I were in the rooms one cold, wet Thursday night before training. I wasn't particularly looking forward to getting out amongst it, and Scotty wasn't either. He went up to Reidy and said, 'I don't feel well, Doc. I've had a stomach-ache all day, and I've been to the toilet twice in the last half-hour. I think I must have eaten something dodgy.'

Doc Reid took one look at him and said, 'C'mon, Scotty. It would be so much easier if you guys just said you didn't feel like training, instead of telling me stories. Go on, out you go.'

'But I really am sick,' protested Scotty.

'You're okay,' said Reidy firmly. 'Off you go.'

Dejected, Scotty turned towards the door. As he passed me I said out of the corner of my mouth, 'Amateur, watch this.'

Unsung heroes

I got to the bench and levered myself up, grimacing, and sat there drawing shallow, feeble breaths.

'What's the problem, Fish?' asked Reidy.

'Don't know, Doc,' I replied. 'I just feel ordinary. My stomach's upset, I'm pooing through the eye of a needle and I'm a bit wobbly on my feet.'

'Let's take a look. Lie down.'

As I lay down I winced. 'Sorry, Doc, my stomach is a bit sore from when I was throwing up during the day. Can you find out what's wrong and give me a shot to stop the nausea? Then I can go out and just run laps.'

'I don't think so, Fish,' said the doc. 'I think we might keep you in here tonight. No sense in risking you for the weekend.'

The look on Scotty's face was priceless, but he knew he had learned at the feet of the master.

BALLOONS

Football clubs are often blessed with generous benefactors, people who have a bit of money and are happy to put it into the club in the form of sponsorships and the like. They expect very little in return, love the players and are pleased to see the club prosper. 'Heymo' was just that sort of person. He was extremely generous and well liked by everyone. Heymo used to host a gathering in the week of the Grand Final, which was very popular among the boys.

I remember a time when one of our senior players had missed a final due to a particularly nasty ankle sprain (or at least that was his version), and Doc Reid was convinced it wouldn't stand up to the next game, which was the Preliminary Final. Sheeds was always pedantic about players being fully fit in finals and Doc never took any unnecessary risks, so the player just had to cop it on the chin. Unfortunately for our shattered hero, it would have been his last game of the year, as the Bombers were knocked out of the race for the flag that week. It was Mad Monday party time – not celebration time, but a chance to let our hair down after a long campaign. Heymo went all out, with a marquee on his tennis court, fully catered spit roast, full bar service, stage and band, the lot. The party started slowly, but then everyone began to realise there was nothing we could do about the year. It was over, and we might as

Unsung heroes

well accept it and move on. The drinks started to flow and everyone got into it.

One of our guys actually worked for Heymo and had a mole in the system who could assist in a supply of alcohol not accessible over the bar. Our guy went inside and helped himself to a few top-shelf bottles of spirits, brought them out and then hid them so that only he and a select few, including the injured star, had access to them.

As the rest of the team got slowly drunk on beer, off in a dark corner of the marquee a section of the party was finding a gear that surprised most of the other revellers. Our 'insiders' enjoyed the additional company of Johnnie Walker and Jim Beam, old mates from way back. After a couple of hours the bloke who had been unable to play finals football was feeling no pain. His ankle injury was forgotten and he found himself up on stage with a teammate, doing their best Bill and Ted impersonations. They were the life of the party. The other guy was throwing balloons while our star with the crook ankle was pretending to take 'speccies' and generally clowning around.

After a few minutes he looked down to see that just about everyone had left, except for one person. Sitting bang in front of the stage, with his face in his hands, was Sheedy. He was watching his injured match-winner, the bloke whose ankle had been too bad to play in a Preliminary Final, mucking around the stage marking balloons. He didn't understand that the star's ankle was so sore that, sober, he couldn't have walked, but pissed, he was a champion.

To this day I don't think Kevin believed the player when he tried to explain. In fact, we all remember our hero first trying to blame the doc for poor diagnosis, but then, when that didn't wash, suggesting it was the devil's work – which only served to lose him more credibility. What is it with cynical coaches?

PROPERTY

It was a particularly wet and miserable night back in the winter of 1992 when I arrived for training at Windy Hill. Dark clouds hung overhead, looking more threatening than Dean Wallis charging into a pack of opposition players, and it was colder than an angry Tony Lockett stare.

Getting motivated for training on such a night was one of the more difficult assignments confronting a Bomber player of any era. One man, though, looked forward to these sessions, and that man was our property steward, Ken Betts. 'Bettsy', as he was affectionately known, was as annoying as he was ruthless behind the door to his domain off to one side of the change rooms: annoying because he took great delight in seeing us collect our jumpers and then refusing our requests for long sleeves, and ruthless because he had a memory like an elephant and those who crossed him paid a heavy price for years to come. In fact, one of the most degrading experiences for an Essendon player was having to occasionally suck up to Bettsy to extract something as simple as a towel from him.

Bettsy was a postman by day. A relatively tall man with a face only a mother could love, he had one leg shorter than the other and with a club foot. Consequently he had a boot made that was built up and noticeably smaller than the other. This gave rise to another nickname, 'Scooter'.

Unsung heroes

The door to Bettsy's room resembled *Mr Ed*'s stable door. Behind that door he notoriously had a stash of liquid gold (beer), and only he was allowed anywhere near it. Legend said he also had a garage at home full of priceless Essendon memorabilia, but this was only on the say-so of even less credible types. Bettsy's favourite word was 'No' and sadly it became a habitual part of his vocabulary to the point where one day one of the boys mentioned to a lonely Bettsy that he could set him up with Elle Macpherson – and he still said no! (I said he was annoying and ruthless, not dumb.)

Anyway, back to that wet, miserable night at Windy Hill. Bettsy had arrived early that afternoon and partaken in a few 'sherbets' to loosen himself up for what promised to be a torrid evening of cold, grumpy footballers. He was his usual self, giving the boys a hard time over just about everything and clearly under the influence of one too many. Eventually Sheeds approached the 'stables' and requested the coach's official all-weather jacket, the one with the sponsor logo plastered all over it that Sheeds had to wear under instruction from the club.

By this point the boys were more than a little annoyed with Bettsy and were hurling abuse and generally giving him a hard time. It was hysterical stuff, and served to take our minds off training for a few minutes, so a lot of attention was paid to the Sheedy v. Bettsy encounter. It went something like this.

'Can I have my jacket please, Ken?' asked Kev.

'No!'

'Give me my jacket, Bettsy,' demanded Kev.

'No,' said Bettsy.

'Stop stuffing around and give me my bloody jacket!'

'No!' came the defiant, alcohol-induced response. A crowd had gathered by this time, with everyone enjoying the Mexican stand-off and cranking up Bettsy.

'Listen, Ken, stop stuffing around and get my bloody jacket now!' bellowed Sheeds.

Property

'No, you can't have it,' Ken said, obviously not realising he was now officially taking his life into his hands. The boys loved it, but it was getting uglier by the second.

'Why can't I have my bloody jacket?'

'Because you didn't ask nicely,' was the witty retort.

'Yes, I did!'

'No, you didn't!' By now it had descended into a schoolyard verbal toe-to-toe and the crowd was lapping it up.

'Right, if you don't give me my jacket I'm coming in to get it myself, and I'll give you a clip under the ear for good measure!' shouted a fed-up Sheeds (or something to that effect, only a little more colourful).

'You're not allowed in here,' retorted Bettsy indignantly.

'That does it!' Sheeds leapt over the half-door, lucky not to throw his back out in the process, and went at Bettsy. There's a theory that Bettsy's bad breath may have saved his life, because no sooner did Sheeds have the upper hand than he bounced off, grabbed his jacket and stormed out the door. Bettsy just stood there in shock, probably more because no one had ever been on his turf before and got away with it than because he had just put the coach off side.

Sheeds yelled at us to get on the track and we all charged out, forgetting it was near subzero temperatures and just wanting to please the boss. The steam coming from his ears would have kept half of us warm for the night if he'd been up for it. Bettsy had got him so worked up that we trained until what seemed like midnight. It was a tough session and Sheeds scowled all the way through it. It was entirely Scooter's fault, which didn't endear him to the boys. We made sure that his job was very difficult for a long time after that, not returning gear, returning just one sock so as to muck up his beloved pairings, jumping in and out of his 'stables' and generally making his life a misery.

Bettsy loved the club and his job, but lacked people skills. He was a popular character at Essendon until his retirement

Unsung heroes

in the mid-1990s, and a loyal club servant who, for the most part, got the respect he deserved – even if sometimes he got tired and emotional on the back of a couple of coldies and picked the wrong target to mess with.

***

ANDY ANGWIN WAS the property steward at Hawthorn. A former Best and Fairest winner and fellow number 4 wearer at Hawthorn, as well as a man with a slightly warped sense of humour, he and I hit it off. Nothing was ever a problem for Andy, or so I thought. Underneath that angelic (if a little worn and weather-beaten) exterior lay a heart that fed off mischief and often got up to no good.

Being late for training isn't looked upon lightly The coach can yell and scream all he wants, but for some players it just doesn't sink in, and this is where Andy would dispense his own unique justice. The steward's room is where the gear – shorts, jumpers etc. – is kept for training; we only had to bring our shoes. The reason for keeping the training gear there was to make sure we had clothes to train in. It was surprising how many players turned up unable to train because they had 'forgotten' their kit. Late players would enter the steward's room and race straight to Andy, saying, 'Mate, I'm late. I need shorts and a jumper. What have you got?'

Andy would look them straight in the eye and reply with a jovial, 'No worries, kid. Here you go.'

'Thanks, Andy. You're a lifesaver,' and they'd rush off to change. To punish them for being late, though, Andy would

Property

sometimes give them shorts that were two or three sizes too small. This gave the boys two options: incur the wrath of the coach by being even later, or run around in shorts that gave you a lump in your throat or caused one wheel to fall off your bike. Neither was pleasant, but both were far less painful than facing the coach.

After training, hot water, shower space and a dry towel were as hard to find as a straight answer during question time in Parliament. One afternoon some of the boys raced into the rooms, stripped down and then opened their lockers to find Andy had replaced the towels with face washers – dry, fluffy, perfectly folded face washers. For most of them it was annoying, but I think Jason Dunstall was quite happy. Jason is the only person I know who likes to use those tiny soaps from a motel because they make everything seem bigger, if you know what I mean. The face washer was no different. He proudly walked around with it, yelling out to anyone who would listen, 'Hey look! No hands.'

ACE

WHEN I STARTED playing for the Bombers I was still living at home in Ringwood, in Melbourne's outer east, so the club would send a taxi to pick me up. Ringwood to Essendon on its own was enough to make any cabbie sit an extra six inches back from the steering wheel, but in this case, the driver also had to pick up recruits from Mitcham, Vermont, Heatherdale and Blackburn.

The man entrusted with this precious cargo was a cabbie called 'Ace', and he worshipped the ground we walked on. Sadly, this wasn't because we were league footballers – I don't think Ace cared what we did for a living. No, he loved us because we were a cash cow. Three times a week he made the return trip from Ringwood to Essendon via Mitcham, Vermont, Heatherdale and Blackburn. I believe – and this is not an exaggeration – that his fares for the year totalled in the vicinity of $40 000.

I didn't realise what an influence Ace and those three return cab rides a week were having on me until I got my L-plates. Like most kids I pestered Dad to take me out in the family car, and after a fair bit of resistance he finally relented. I'll never forget the horrified look on his face when I slid into the driver's seat, adjusted the mirror so I could see Mum in the back, wound the window down and put my arm out, put my left leg

Ace

up on the tunnel between the bucket seats and, without a moment's hesitation, swung into the traffic without signalling or even looking to see if anything was coming.

The trip to Essendon with Ace took about one and a half hours, which is a long time to keep the attention of five teenage boys. Usually, not long after the trip had started, the windows would be down and we'd be yelling constructive criticism on people's appearance to them as we drove past. Every few weeks we would be called into the recruiting manager's office, where he would sit us down and talk to us about our responsibilities, not only to ourselves but to the club, how our actions reflected badly on both, and not to do it any more, blah, blah, blah. We'd restrain ourselves for a few cab trips and then it would start again, gaining momentum until another concerned member of the public went to the trouble of jotting down the time and the cab rego and phoning the cab company to make a complaint.

Things were a little different on the way home. See, on the way home we had no real time schedule and weren't in as much of a rush. So you had five hungry young footballers heading home in a cab they weren't paying for, with a driver who would have taken them to Alice Springs if he thought he could get away with it. Some nights I think the fare to Alice Springs may have been cheaper. We would leave Essendon and head to Collingwood for fish and chips, then off to a video parlour in Brunswick to play the latest video games. All the time the meter would be ticking. After the games parlour Ace would bundle us back into the car and take us to his favourite haunt, an adult bookshop in the city. There were some advantages to being young and having nobody know who you were. I couldn't do anything like that now; thank goodness for the Internet. Some nights it would take a couple of hours to get home and the cost would be astronomical. I think back now and wonder why nobody ever thought to compare the fare out with the fare in.

Unsung heroes

One Thursday night on the way to Essendon, Ace let slip that he was a Bruce Lee fan. He copped a lot of ribbing from us because after his years of driving a cab, we doubted Ace could run out of sight on a dark night. His idea of exercise would have been wiping the chip crumbs off the front of his pyjamas before he reached for the telly remote. Anyway, he went on and on all the way to Windy Hill: Bruce Lee this, Bruce Lee that. After training we came out and Ace was there waiting, as always, so we jumped in and told him to take us to the Coburg drive-in, where they were screening a Bruce Lee movie.

We watched the entire movie from the cab, and the only thing that spoiled the night was the audible click of the meter every thirty seconds. It would have been cheaper for us all to go to Gold Class at Crown and have a meal at Cecconi's afterwards – but of course that wasn't an option back then. The whole time Ace was watching the movie, I'm sure he was trying to work out how he could somehow add his admission price onto the fare. He never liked to let a chance go by.

MICROWAVE

When I was a young footballer and still living at home, I would come back from training laughing like a drain and full of food. Mum and Dad would be sitting watching the telly. Mum would save some of whatever they'd had for tea and put it on a plate, cover it with foil and sit it on a pot of simmering water on top of the stove, for me to have when I got home.

After three and a half hours of this the whole meal had usually turned a uniform grey colour. The congealed gravy could have filled holes in the asphalt on the Hume, the peas – there were always peas, never any other green vegetable – had gone like ball bearings, the carrot rings had turned up at the edges, and the mashed spuds had had any moisture sucked right out of them. It was horrible, but I had no choice but to eat it. No young boy likes to hurt his mother's feelings, and nothing hurt Mum's feelings more than my refusing to eat the meat and three veg she'd prepared.

After my first season I decided to make life easier for Mum and bought her a microwave. (Microwaves are a marvellous time-saving invention – most houses now wouldn't be without them. However, I hadn't realised until a few weeks ago how fast-paced our lives have become. When I was a young kid growing up I remember Mum standing in front of a saucepan of peas waiting for them to cook. She'd have her apron on and a tea towel or spoon in her hand and she'd be looking at the pot and saying, 'Cook! Come on, cook, will you?' Sometimes they'd just start to boil and she'd whip them off the stove and say, 'That'll do. I haven't got all night.' Well, the other night I came home and Jo was standing in front of the microwave. She was staring at it and watching the peas go around in a cup, saying, 'Come on, come on! Hurry up and cook!' With about ten seconds to go she pushed the 'open door' button, the bell dinged, and she said, 'That'll do. I haven't got all night.')

Now where were we? Oh yes, the microwave I bought for Mum. Let me just hasten to add that I didn't buy it for Mother's Day. I remember when a 'new father' friend of mine brought his wife a frypan for Mother's Day. Luckily for him it was Teflon-coated, and the proctologist he saw said it should be easy to remove. Anyway, Mum was a little reluctant to use her new appliance, but I told her it would save time and make it easy to reheat my meals at night after training (anything to escape the dried-up mess that was dinner). Eventually she agreed to try it. That night I finished training and after the usual shenanigans on the way home got in the door at about 9.30. I went into the kitchen and Mum yelled out that my dinner was in the microwave. Sure enough, spinning around was my dinner. I opened the door to take it out, and sitting on the plate was a horrid dry mess. I would have needed an ice pick to break the mashed spuds and a jackhammer for the gravy. To this day I don't know what kind of meat it was.

'Mum,' I said, 'what happened?'

'Nothing, dear. I cooked your tea with ours at about six, then I covered it with Glad Wrap like you said and put it in the microwave on low until you got home.'

For the next few years our microwave was nothing more than a very expensive digital clock. But I have to give credit where credit is due: Mum really tried to embrace the new technology.

Microwave

One afternoon I rang her from training and asked if I could bring two mates home for her famous lamb roast dinner. She said sure, but then remembered that the only lamb leg she had was frozen. Now Mum doesn't drive (in fact, God bless her, she has never had a driver's licence – she believes that she married a chauffeur, so why bother?), so she couldn't get to the butchers.

Remember the movie *Airport '77*? The pilots are unable to fly the plane – I don't remember why – and a stewardess takes the controls for landing. The air traffic controllers have to talk her down step by step. That's the best way to explain what happened next. I had to talk Mum through defrosting the leg of lamb. She fetched the meat and brought it to the microwave, then I got her to find the weight on the label and explained how to enter it into the number pad so the meat would defrost perfectly. We accomplished this fairly easily, and I heard a lot of beeping and figured everything was okay. I told Mum I'd see her in a few hours.

On the drive home I waxed lyrical about how good the roast was going to be. All boys think their mum makes the best roast, but my mum's really was (and still is) superb. I built it up to be something out of this world, and the three of us hit the back door and burst into the kitchen like corks from champagne bottles. Then we stopped dead in our tracks – the microwave door was ajar and half a leg of lamb was hanging out of it while Mum stood there pushing the buttons and scratching her head. I hadn't thought to ask if she'd been able to shut the door on the meat, and she hadn't realised you had to. She turned to me and said, 'The damn thing really is useless, Paul. I've been trying since you hung up but I can't get it to work.' We had a lovely pizza that night, though, so all wasn't lost.

The microwave still sits gathering dust on a shelf in Mum and Dad's spare room, a monument to Mum's proud and defiant refusal to enter the late twentieth century.

THE PSYCH

WHEN I FIRST started to play league football, coach Kevin Sheedy would yell at us for a few hours three times a week and then we'd play on Saturday and he'd yell at us some more. Actually, it was better on a Saturday because he'd send a runner out to yell at us instead. Having a runner relay messages isn't always that successful. Sheeds would bark orders to the runners so often that there were times they had no idea what the message was. On a number of occasions our runner came out and said, 'I have no idea what he said – just do something a bit different to what you're doing now. Okay?'

(I often wonder about runners. Have you ever seen the TV news when they get a translator on to translate what a foreign despot or tyrant is saying? Is the translator in fact relaying exactly what the leader said, or are they toning it down or beefing it up, depending on how they think the situation should be handled? Runners have that power, and it's well known that they like nothing better than to get players into strife. It's all fun to them.)

Football clubs nowadays have all sorts of experts on hand to deal with just about any situation that might crop up. Coaching staff have become very specialised: we have ruck coaches, forward-line coaches, back-line coaches and goal-kicking coaches. There are fitness experts, running coaches,

The psych

weight specialists and all sorts of ancillary experts, such as dieticians, counsellors and psychologists.

In the early 1980s the chance of having any sort of specialist at a football club was pretty remote. Essendon, however, have always been innovators in this sort of thing and in the early to mid-1980s we found ourselves with a resident psychologist. His name was Rudi Webster and he was a West Indian who had done some work with Richmond previously (which is where Sheeds got to know him), as well as extensive work with the West Indies cricket team. Rudi was actually qualified in radiotherapy, not psychology, but he was very good at his chosen craft. When Mark Harvey found out about Rudi's other talent he was overjoyed and brought in a Sony Walkman to be fixed. Rudi had to explain to him what a radiotherapist actually did, and Harvs was very disappointed.

Rudi had had a great deal of success with a certain technique he'd tried with the West Indians: group hypnotherapy. He decided to try it with us, too, and arranged with Sheeds to take a number of players out of conventional training to go to his house in Kooyong for a session. Rudi was very excited by the fact that most of the team took him up on his offer. Truth be known, it was halfway through the season and the middle of winter, and we would have done just about anything to get out of running around the track at Windy Hill.

We all arrived at Rudi's place, a magnificent home full of all sorts of cricket memorabilia, and made our way into his living room, where we found beanbags, couches and mattresses on the floor. He let us get comfortable, put on some ambient music and closed the curtains.

So Rudi, who thought we were there for enlightenment, now had a group of excitable young footballers who had really gathered for the express reason of escaping training. It was a recipe for disaster.

Unsung heroes

He started to talk to us in a slow, low, comforting voice. 'I want you to close your eyes. Close your eyes and relax, relax, relax. I want you to visualise a garden, a beautiful garden with many magnificent flowers just slightly bending in the wind . . .'

A voice piped up. It was Michael Thomson, who happened to have a gardening business. 'What sort of flowers, Rudi?'

'Pardon?'

'What sort of flowers are they?' asked Michael.

'Does it matter?'

'I suppose not. I'd just like to know.'

Slightly angry, Rudi replied, 'Sunflowers. They are tall sunflowers.'

'Good-oh.'

'Picture the flowers stretching all the way to the horizon. On the horizon there are clouds.'

'Are they rain clouds?' someone asked.

'No, they are not rain clouds. They are clouds.'

'Probably cumulonimbus.'

'What?' asked a now-exasperated Rudi.

'Probably cumulonimbus,' said the voice. 'Those big clouds that look like rain but mostly they are too high.'

'No,' said another voice, 'that's cumulostratus. They're the high ones, cumulo——'

'That's enough!' snapped Rudi. 'They are clouds, white fluffy clouds. Now please concentrate.'

'Okay,' we all murmured.

'All right,' continued Rudi, 'now imagine you are lying in the garden, the sun is warming you and you are starting to feel very relaxed. I want you to let go and relax, just relax . . .'

Someone obviously became too relaxed, because just then there was a *brrraaaaap*, like the sound of someone tearing a sheet. This was followed by what sounded like someone letting air out of a balloon while they held the opening slightly

The psych

closed – sort of a high-pitched *brrrrrrrrrp*. To this day I don't know who it was, but very soon afterwards it became apparent that something had died inside him the day before. The boys just couldn't help themselves and started sniggering, snorting and then laughing outright.

Rudi was by now at the end of his tether. 'If you are not going to take this seriously then I want you to go. Just leave now!' That was all we needed. We were up and off like a shot.

My last recollection of the day was Rudi standing as everyone ran past him to freedom, yelling, 'This never happened back home! I had respect there! People took this seriously!'

And Mark Harvey stopped and said, 'Rudi, you need to relax. Don't get uptight. Hypnotherapy, that's what you need.' Then he slipped quickly out the door.

IN THE FIRST game of the 1984 season, we were playing St Kilda at Moorabbin. Rudi approached me before the game and asked in his strong West Indian accent, 'How are you feeling today, Paul?'

I replied, 'I feel great. Ready to kick a bag, Rudi.' Bear in mind I was nineteen, this was my first game at full-forward and, although a touch misguided, I was very, very confident.

Rudi was horrified. 'Oh no, no, no, no, Paul,' he said, sitting down next to me. 'You can't think like that. You can't afford to get ahead of yourself. This is a long journey; it takes many small steps. Setting goals is admirable, but if they are too

Unsung heroes

high and you do not achieve them it may leave you feeling a little disappointed after the game.'

He went on, 'My advice to you is to adopt the thinking of Viv Richards: keep it simple early, go for the ones and the twos and wait until you take the shine off the ball.' I didn't want to point out that there are no twos in football, just goals and behinds, but if it was good enough for Viv, then I'd take Rudi's advice.

A few minutes later I ran onto the ground and took my spot at full-forward. The ball cleared the centre bounce and was kicked to the forward line, I took a mark and goaled within two minutes. By half-time I had a few more goals and was feeling pretty good, having followed Rudi's advice. I was sitting on the bench in front of the lockers in the rooms, relatively at ease with my game, when Rudi came over.

'Paul,' he said.

'Yes?'

'I've been watching you out there today.'

'Yes?'

'Remember the advice I gave you?'

'Yes, but I've been——'

'No, no, no, don't worry. I want you to go out there now and play your shots. Let's see some fours and sixes!'

TOUCHY-FEELY

GETTING A RUBDOWN or massage, or 'myotherapy' as they like to call it these days, can be one of the highlights of a footballer's week. Your tired, sore body can take respite on a bench for thirty or so minutes and let the magic hands of the qualified trainer do his or her thing.

The men and women who perform this duty at a football club have come a long way since I first started, and are now very proficient at hitting the right spots. This hasn't always been the case. I'm positive that some guys, in the early days in particular, were thrown a bottle of oil and had no real idea of what to do next. In fact, I once saw a trainer applying the oil to himself before training, like the players do before a game. He looked great glistening in the afternoon sun that day, but I think he missed the point!

It's very common for players to develop a relationship with their preferred masseur and make sure they always get rubbed down by them. This could be seen as playing favourites, but when it comes to the right level of pressure there can be no compromising. However, it's the masseurs who were avoided that I would like to tell you about here, as they make the average ones seem like God's gift to massage. Mind you, I should also point out that I never met a bad bloke; in fact I respected and liked just about every trainer I came into contact with.

Unsung heroes

I don't want to offend any of these great servants of football, so they shall remain nameless.

There was the one who used to lather up his 'victim' in a bath of oil so that the masseur's hands would virtually freestyle across the player's torso with consummate ease. This had absolutely no effect whatsoever on the player, other than to ensure it took several days to remove all the oil. Not effective, but very sensual!

Speaking of sensual, there was one guy back in the 1980s who would head straight for your hamstrings and proceed to work them over like there was no tomorrow. The only problem was that, because the hamstring runs high up into the buttock, his hands would often stray into areas best left well alone. In fact, there was the odd occasion when a player would find the hands coming way too close to the 'no-go zone' for comfort, at which point the session would be brought to an abrupt halt. We usually saved this bloke for the new guys for a bit of a welcome to club stuff.

One of my favourites was the masseur who felt he could diagnose just about any ailment by playing with your feet. Now I know there's a link between the feet and other parts of the body, but this guy was ahead of his time and took the theory to a whole new level. I recall he was working on my feet once when he asked if I was experiencing any difficulty with my performance. I said, 'Yeah, I can't get a bloody kick at the moment.' He said, 'No, not that kind of performance.' I asked him what he was talking about, never twigging what he was referring to, and he said, 'In the sack'.

He was very serious and concerned for me, but I assured him I was still the machine I had always been (it's my book, so I'll say what I want) and not to worry. He said he would like to keep an eye on it, as there was definitely something there. Well, this sort of feedback can have a devastating effect on one so young and impressionable as I was, and I went

Touchy-feely

home to my beautiful wife and made a conscious effort to lift my game. Seventeen years of marriage later, I'm confident that what he felt in my foot that fateful day was possibly my capacity to 'perform' for only six days a week. Every man needs a day to himself to regroup, doesn't he?

The worst nightmare for any player who is trying to escape the pressures and demands of the sport on the rubdown bench, is confronting those trainers who genuinely believe they are funny. It could be argued that this applies to most trainers, but some are much worse than others, I can assure you. Now I love a good laugh as much as the next bloke, but time and place are the keys, without a shadow of a doubt, and it was the trainers with no sense of timing who left themselves wide open to an unexpected response from a player wanting some 'own time'.

One of the funnier incidents involved a down-on-form, just-flogged-on-the-training-track player and a just-finished-work-had-a-great-day trainer. In staggered the player to the trainer's room, looking for some respite from a world where everyone seemed out to get him. Mister Not-a-Care-in-the-World jumped up and invited the player to lie on his stomach so he could get to work. The player wanted to drift off and leave his worries behind for a little while; the trainer wanted to share what was great about life and throw in a few gags for good measure. The upbeat, one-way nature of the conversation, mixed with the worst gags ever told within the walls of a football club (even allowing for some of my own), turned into a recipe for disaster.

The player, who gave the trainer repeated hints of his desire just to relax and not be disturbed – which the trainer chose to ignore on the basis of 'How could he not be enjoying my company? I'm a crack-up' – finally had enough. He rolled off the bench (he was still physically wrecked), grabbed his pillow and proceeded to give the trainer a volley of blows to the head

Unsung heroes

and body. It was harmless but very cathartic, and quickly escalated into a free-for-all as the trainer decided to defend himself and other players and trainers came to assist. The lines became very blurred as to who was helping whom, but that didn't seem to matter much in the end. It surely had to be the biggest pillow fight in AFL history, as numbers swelled to include unsuspecting passers-by. It eventually subsided and the offending instigators were left to ponder what had got seriously out of control.

A player with no energy left in the tank and a trainer who still wanted to get out the punchline to his last joke, which had been ruined by a swift blow to the head with a pillow, stood there looking at one another from opposite sides of the bench. In that moment of reflection, the player decided he still wanted his rub and the trainer decided he would come back to that punchline another day. Not a word was spoken, yet a compromise was reached.

A valuable lesson was learned that day by all involved: no matter how bad the joke, always get the punchline out before the first blow of the pillow!

MINDER

No matter what you think of Kevin Sheedy and some of the things he has done over the years, there's no argument that he's been great for the Essendon Football Club and the game in general. I have always had the utmost respect for him and for what he puts into the promotion of football, but there's another lesser-known side to Kevin that makes him very special and unique, and that is the size of his heart. The amount of time and effort he has put into charity over the years is staggering. Some of his work is acknowledged, but he does most of it with no fuss and fanfare because it's just who he is and he doesn't expect anything in return.

Being as busy as Kevin has been over the years, and with his tendency to say yes to everything and everyone, the club deemed it necessary in the mid-1990s to appoint a minder for Sheeds, someone who could take care of his diary and ensure he managed all his commitments – in particular, his coaching commitments.

Arguably the biggest godsend for everyone who has dealt with Sheeds since then has been Jeanette Curwood, who was appointed to that role. Jeanette is a wonderful person who rules Kev with an iron fist and protects him like a guardian angel. She hasn't necessarily cured him of his habitual lateness, but she has managed to answer the question that's on the lips

Unsung heroes

of everyone at Essendon at one time or another: 'Where's Sheeds?' Now you need only pick up the phone and ask Jeanette where he is. I'm sure she has a better idea than even Sheeds' wife, Geraldine!

Jeanette recounted a story of her first week working for the man she affectionately calls 'a walking organisational nightmare', which sums him up beautifully. She arrived at work on her first day to find a diary she couldn't follow and a list of engagements that had her thinking there must be more than one Kevin Sheedy. One of the issues to be resolved was the whereabouts of some cricket bats Sheeds had sold at various recent charity auctions but that had not yet materialised. All she knew of the bats was that people from the charities were chasing them up, and some mysterious markings in Sheeds' diary: 'B.B.B. bats'.

Jeanette had to know more, so she headed into his office to get to the bottom of the problem. 'Kevin, what can you tell me about these cricket bats?' she asked.

'What cricket bats?' came Sheeds' reply.

'The ones you've marked "B.B.B." in your diary.'

'Oh,' said Kev. 'They're the Bradman–Border–Benaud-signed cricket bats I've sold at auctions recently and made lots of money for cancer research and other charities.'

'How many have you sold?' Jeanette wanted to know.

'Seven,' was Kev's justifiably proud response.

'Well, where are they so I can send them off?'

'Haven't got 'em yet,' said Sheeds. He'd sold seven cricket bats that he'd never had, signed by three of Australia's sporting icons whom he'd never approached. It was classic Sheeds – well intentioned but lacking in organisation.

'How are we going to get them?' Jeanette inquired.

'Don't worry – we'll get 'em,' said a confident Sheeds. Jeanette knew that the great Don Bradman lived in Adelaide, and Allan Border was in Queensland, and to top it all off, the doyen of cricket broadcasting, Richie Benaud, was known to be very hard to catch – and that was when he was in Australia. All this on her first day!

It took poor Jeanette ten months to secure the signatures, first buying the bats and then sending them around the country to each 'B'. It was her first taste of what lay ahead in her job as the personal assistant of a man whom many believed was unassistable, but it was also a baptism of fire that would hold her in good stead for the future. She still works with Kevin, and together they form one of the great Australian sporting partnerships. She has since learned not to worry too much about his promises because, as Kevin always says, when it comes to the crunch, 'We'll get 'em'!

PART 6
TELLY
TALES

SOUND EFFECTS

OVER THE PAST few years, on Sunday mornings during the footy season, I've been lucky enough to be involved with *Rex Hunt's Footy Panel* on Channel 7. It's great fun and I love being a part of it. Because it's totally unscripted, you have to be on your toes. Anything can happen, and quite often it does.

For those who haven't been involved with television, I'll try and explain how it works. The set for the show is in the studio. On the floor are camera operators, a make-up person, a few other odds and sods, and a floor manager. The show is directed from a booth above the set and the director speaks to the camera operators and floor manager via a walkie-talkie. The sound is controlled from a booth next to the director's booth. As people speak, the sound guy brings the appropriate microphone into play.

There's a fair amount of fun and frivolity before, during and after the show. Prior to the start you go to wardrobe to make sure that what you're wearing doesn't strobe (upset the camera) or clash with another presenter. After wardrobe you head off to make-up, where you get powdered down to stop you shining, then it's on to audio where you have your radio mic put on. These are the little microphones you see on the lapels of presenters' jackets, or on the front of their shirts. Hidden on your body somewhere, usually on the back of your pants, is a control box where the mic is switched on and off. Then it's just a matter of waiting until you're called to the set.

One Sunday morning we were sitting on the set and the floor manager had given us the nod that there were five minutes to go. A young Geelong player who was joining us for the first time leaned over and said he was just going to the toilet. He left the set and wandered off and after about thirty seconds the sound of a door opening and closing echoed through the studio speakers. This was followed by the sound of a zipper and pants hitting the ground as a toilet seat dropped. What followed was a cacophony of noises that, frankly, were nothing short of embarrassing. As there was nobody in the sound booth to turn his mic down, we had the benefit of full studio-quality sound on the best radio mics available.

There was absolutely nothing any of us could do. We tried talking louder to drown out the sound, but that didn't work. It was a long couple of minutes, and we were all relieved when we heard the sound of paper being scrunched (which surprised me, because I had always assumed the guy was a folder) and the toilet being flushed. He returned to the studio, took his place at the desk, looked at the bemused expressions on our faces and said, 'What? What's wrong?'

The floor manager yelled across to us, 'One minute, guys. Oh, and son, you need a bit more fibre in your diet, I think.'

During the breaks our young Cat kept asking, 'What did he mean by that?' After the show the sound guy came into the dressing room and gave him the tape, which we promptly put on for him to listen to.

He never appeared on the show again, but somehow the story got out and he copped a lot of ribbing on the ground from opponents for the rest of the season. Poor bloke had to put up with comments like, 'Hey mate, who does number two work for?' and, 'Before you kick, why don't you bite your lip and give it hell?'

SIMON AND LOU

ONE OF THE great men, and great characters, of football with whom I had the pleasure of playing is my long-time rucking nemesis and good mate, Simon Madden. For some unknown and totally inexplicable reason we would more often than not be roomed together on interstate trips. This was a nightmare for two blokes over 200 cm, as no hotel room in the world contains two king-size beds. It was always a battle to get first hands on the key and then a physical test of strength to be the first into the room to claim the larger bed. Often it was the elder statesman who won out, and I have many memories of sleeping on the floor, or with my legs dangling over the end of my single bed, like Humpty Dumpty on his brick wall.

At first I thought it was someone's idea of a practical joke to room us together, but after it happened a couple of times it crossed my mind that it could be Sheeds trying to fast-track my development. I don't know how being kept awake by Simon's snoring or tolerating his disregard for wind-breaking protocols was going to help me become a better footballer. Anyway, it eventually became apparent that it was purely an administrative bungle that had been allowed to go on for too long.

One such occasion was a trip to Perth to represent Victoria, back in 1990. As the flight from Melbourne was a long one and we had to play the next day, massages were offered to the players upon our arrival at the team hotel. Simon and I went to our room, which on this trip was at the Perth International Hotel, and prepared to decide the issue. We had played together for about eight years at this stage and had progressed our conflict resolution to a fair game of rock, scissors, paper (best of three, of course). I lost yet again – it had to be rigged – and set up camp in the single bed made to order for one of Snow White's little friends.

After Simon had finished gloating about how comfortable his queen-size was, he suggested we head up to the rooftop gym and pool for a quick rubdown to loosen our tired, stiff muscles, and in my case strained ones from trying to fit on the bloody bed.

We arrived to find the massage benches free, so we quickly dropped our trackies and jumped on. Naturally enough we wanted the works, so it was into the birthday suit and on with a towel to protect our dignity. A short while later we heard the door open behind us and a group of people bowling up to where we were being rubbed down. Suddenly, a very recognisable voice announced his arrival: it was the great Lou Richards, who was there covering the game for Channel 9. 'Hey, boys!' bellowed Lou. 'Mind if I get a grab for the news?'

'No worries,' replied Simon. 'Make sure the camera angle is okay, though.'

'You'll be right. I'm the best in the business, a thorough professional,' said a typically modest Lou.

While Lou was off to the side painstakingly rehearsing his lines, the audio boys miked Simon and me for the segment. They didn't have small lapel microphones, only the normal ones you commonly see used in TV interviews. We were lying on our backs, so they placed them carefully beside us, under our towels and pretty much in line with our hips, where they would be out of sight. Our instructions were simple: hold onto your mic and keep it out of view of the cameras.

Simon and Lou

It wasn't long before Lou came back, ready for action. 'Righto, Simon,' he said. 'I'm just going to stand here next to you, lightly rubbing your leg as if I'm giving you a massage, while I do my bit to camera. I'll then throw a question at you for a quick answer. Whaddya say?'

'Sounds good to me, Louie,' said Simon. 'Just watch what you're doing with those hands, hey?'

'You'll be right, son,' replied Lou.

The cameraman indicated he was ready to go and called, 'Action!' Lou slipped into gear.

'Thanks, Tony, we're over here in beautiful Perth on top of the Perth International Hotel, getting ready for the big game between Victoria and Western Australia.' As Lou was going through his opener, rubbing Simon's leg, Simon slowly edged his microphone up over his thigh under the towel. Oblivious to this, Lou continued. 'And with me, Tony, are two of the biggest men in football, Paul Salmon and Simon Madden. Well, Simon, how am I going?' he said, referring to his prowess as a masseur.

Simon had by this time manoeuvred the microphone into a position that indicated quite obviously that the rub was exciting him more than expected. Straight-faced, he responded, 'You're working wonders for me, Louie!'

At this, Lou looked down to see what could only be described as the result of way too much Viagra. Everyone cracked up, but a dumbfounded Louie could only stammer, 'Um . . . ahh . . .'

The cameraman yelled 'Cut!' and it was a few minutes before everyone was composed enough to get the interview started again.

This time, a sound man lay under the bench, holding our microphones.

BIG SCREEN

THE MOST HORRIFIC incident in season 2002 occurred in the game between Fremantle and Essendon at Subiaco in Round 6. In an accidental collision with teammate Mark McVeigh, James Hird severely damaged his face, requiring delicate and painstaking major surgery that would decide whether he was to play football again.

I was injured that week and was sitting at home in Melbourne watching the game when it happened. My first, selfish reaction was to wonder whether one of my comeback aims – to play with Jim again – would now happen. My thoughts then turned to his family and how his wife, Tanya, and his parents must be feeling. There wasn't a lot any of us could do from the other side of the country, except wait to hear news of his condition and hope everything turned out okay.

I put in calls to Doc Reid and various teammates, but no one knew much. It was too early to tell what the consequences would be, or the extent of the injuries, so I went to bed hoping to find out more in the morning. As it turned out, I didn't have to wait that long.

I was in a deep sleep, dreaming of taking a match-winning screamer in the goal square (we footballers never grow up), when the phone rang. This was really unusual. My three children were all under the age of fourteen and safe at home, so

Big screen

I knew it wasn't one of them saying their car had broken down or, worse, the police telling me one of them was in trouble. However, Jo's mother was in hospital at the time and quite ill. Jo picked up the phone, ghost white.

I heard a voice say, 'Jo, is that you?'

'Yes,' replied Jo.

'It's Reidy here,' said the doc. 'I'm standing next to Hirdy and he wants to talk to Fish.'

'What!' said Jo, angry with Reidy but relieved it wasn't bad news about her mum. 'Are you serious? It's three o'clock in the morning!'

'Well, he's just got out of surgery and says he needs to speak to Fish about something really important,' the doc said.

'Okay then, here he is.' Jo passed me the phone. 'It's Reidy. He says James wants to speak to you about something important.'

I couldn't believe it. The bloke had just come out of major surgery. *Has to be the drugs*, I thought.

I took the phone and said groggily, 'Hirdy?'

'Yeah, Fish. You've gotta do something about the size of the TV in here. It's ridiculous – I can hardly see it from where I am and I know you wouldn't put up with it. It's just not good enough. You must know someone who can help.'

I was a bit more awake now. 'You can't be serious, mate. Doesn't the hospital penthouse have a big-screen TV?' I said, my tongue planted firmly in my cheek. 'That's where *I* usually stay.'

On the other end of the phone there was nothing – just breathing. Apparently, when you leave half your face on someone's knee 3500 kilometres from home, and you've just had surgery that could change your life, you lose a bit of your sense of humour.

I battled on nonetheless. 'Have you at least got your own room?' I asked.

Telly tales

'Yeah, but what about my telly? I can't put up with this. What can you do about it?' Jim demanded.

'Leave it with me, mate. I'm onto it,' I reassured him. We talked about the operation for a while and he told me what he knew, which wasn't a lot. I said I'd be in touch and he handed me back to Reidy.

Laughing, the doc said that after Jim had spoken to Tanya, the first thing he had wanted to do was call me to complain about the TV. 'Obviously he's still under the influence of the anaesthetic and feeling in good spirits, but that will all change pretty soon.' I told him I'd have a go at getting Hirdy a bigger telly, and would keep in touch to follow his progress.

The next day I called back to find that reality had set in and the patient was in some discomfort. Reidy said Jim was having trouble remembering what had taken place the night before. Well, that wasn't going to stop me setting up a practical joke to try and raise his spirits. I called a mate from TEAC, Keith, and asked if he could help me solve Jim's little problem. He said there was someone in Perth who might be able to assist, and made a couple of calls for me. It wasn't long before he rang back to say he had rustled up a big-screen TV that could be delivered to Jim's room.

I would have loved to see the look on Hirdy's face when Keith, who had taken my request for 'the biggest TV in stock' a little too far, rocked up to the hospital in a small removal van, stacked up his trolley, made his way to Jim's room and unloaded a shiny rear-projection TV, surround-sound theatre system and accompanying wall unit. Our clearance from the hospital was only for a large TV, so they got a big surprise as well.

The elements of a successful practical joke are a dash of creativity, a little simplicity and a dose of good timing. This one had everything but the timing. Unfortunately I had overlooked the fact that as painkillers wear off, so too does a patient's sense

Big screen

of humour. So a less-than-welcoming Jim met the TEAC man, and what might have seemed funny a couple of days earlier under the influence of a drip full of methadone was now a badly timed inconvenience.

At least Keith, who is a mad Essendon supporter, is able to tell people he's been told to piss off by James Hird. How many fans can say that?

PART 7
BIG
OCCASIONS

SHADOW-BOXING

My first Grand Final in 1985 was a huge occasion. They say you never forget your first one (surely they mean football), and it's true. It was a day I will remember for the rest of my life, because it was the culmination of so much hard work and so many challenges overcome. I had recently come back from a knee reconstruction and had been playing Reserves footy in Round 21, and the club was going for back-to-back premierships. I had watched in 1984 as my teammates won an exciting Grand Final over Hawthorn, breaking a nineteen-year drought of premiership glory, and seen them gripped by a euphoria I might only ever dream about. It strengthened my resolve to want to be part of something like that one day and share those emotions and successes with them.

With Essendon going in as favourites in 1985, there was plenty for Hawthorn to concern themselves with, not least of which was our very tall forward line. The Hawks decided to bring back veteran champion defender David 'Rubber' O'Halloran for his first game of senior football of 1985, specifically to play on me. An interesting decision given the circumstances, and one that proved to be more than a headache for me early in the game.

Out on the ground everything was as I had expected: adrenaline, intensity, pressure and an amazing atmosphere

Big occasions

created by around 100 000 spectators. I got a good look at the ball early and managed to settle some of my nerves with a few touches and a couple of goals. Down the other end of the ground, Dermott Brereton was strutting around as if the whole crowd had come to see him. Maybe they had. He was an electrifying big-game player, and had a mullet that looked like some sort of elaborate 'rug' – a real crowd-pleaser!

Tensions run very high for the players on these occasions, and back then there were no rules preventing brawls, so it never took much to spark a blue. A lot of people who love football refer to that time as the 'good old days', but I'm not sure it was the best image to be sending overseas or to our kids. Anyway, I remember Michael McCarthy for Hawthorn and my Bomber teammate, the great Leon Baker, having a rather minor altercation on what is now the Southern Stand wing. Before I knew it, players came from everywhere and it turned into an 'all-in', with bodies flying all over the place. It momentarily took me back to Norwood High, when a dropped 20-cent coin in the canteen could turn into a riot as a mob of hungry teenagers pounced with total disregard for their or anyone else's safety. The things you'll do for a vanilla slice!

The 'one in, all in' policy was in full swing in those days, and the boys carried it out to the letter. I took off from the goal square and bolted towards the fray. It mattered little that I had no idea what I was going to do once I got there – flying the flag was all that mattered. As I got closer my mind was racing. Who do I go for? Which bloke is in the most trouble?

Then I saw my teammate Tim Watson in some real strife, valiantly trying to hold two Hawthorn players at bay. They were Russell 'The Fly' Morris, so named because of his social-butterfly exploits, and the notorious champion, my childhood hero and a one-man wrecking machine, 'Lethal' Leigh Matthews. They both had Tim by the throat and were shaking him violently. He needed me now more than ever.

Shadow-boxing

Throughout my career, if my strength wasn't fighting, it had to be decision making. In this case, my decision was as instant as it was astute: I chose Russell. I grabbed him and pulled him to one side, where we shadow-boxed 2 metres apart, daring each other not to come any closer. It was edge-of-your-seat stuff. As I was about to launch myself at Russell and inflict potentially lifelong physical damage (that's my story, anyway), I felt a blow to the back of my head, forceful enough to flip me off my feet and cause my face to make contact with the MCG turf.

By now you have probably either totally forgotten I had an opponent, or you're wondering what had happened to Rubber O'Halloran. Well, he had trailed me into the fight, obviously feeling every bit of his mid-thirtysomething years, and waited for the right moment to poleaxe me with a forearm to the head. I slowly picked myself up off the ground, spitting grass and dirt from my mouth, and staggered back to my position. By the time I got there, play had re-started. It was minutes before I could see with any clarity, because night fell early that day and the stars were beautiful.

A couple of big lessons had been learned that I was never to forget: never lead your opponent into an all-in fight, and always shadow-box with your back to the fence.

FAST-FORWARD FIVE years to 1990 and the now-infamous Essendon v. Collingwood Grand Final. This is the game that ultimately led to new 'mêlée' laws being introduced. It's

Big occasions

nearly quarter-time and Magpie Denis Banks is wrestling with Bomber Kieran Sporn. The siren goes and it escalates into the final scene from the old movie *The Wanderers*, where rival gangs come together for an 'anything goes' fight. Déjà vu for me as players come from everywhere. My opponent is Craig 'Ned' Kelly, the big Magpie strongman and enforcer, and when he sees what's happening his eyes light up like a kid's in a candy store. We momentarily hesitate – why, I'll never know. He looks at me, probably deciding whether to take me out now or later; I look at the fight, then at him, deciding whether it's safer here or over there in amongst the bunfight.

My experience from previous encounters takes over and a voice inside my head tells me to wait for him to make the first move. It's only a few seconds but seems like an eternity before I break the deadlock by saying, 'After you, Ned.' With that, Ned takes off like a dog obeying his master's command, and I have effectively eliminated my biggest threat with three little words.

I get in there and don't know where to start, kind of like a Saturday morning in the garden at home. All I can do is throw bodies and manoeuvre myself through the rubble. It's a victory of sorts, on a day I would rather forget, with Collingwood going on to win its first premiership in thirty-two years, a result that still haunts me.

Rules were changed as a consequence of that fight and we no longer see such ugly scenes in our great game. Unfortunately it also means we are deprived of some great shadow-boxing!

PROCESSION

IT GOES WITHOUT saying that the ultimate goal for any footballer is to play in and win a Grand Final. As a footballer, this is your main focus for the year. In a cruel irony, though, in the week you really need to focus on your goal, many things happen to distract you. There are interviews and TV appearances, and cameras following your every waking move.

In 1993 Essendon came from nowhere to make the Grand Final, and the week leading up to the big day was phenomenal. Our own Gavin Wanganeen won the Brownlow Medal, which switched the spotlight even more firmly onto us. For the older players who had been through it before it was harrowing enough, but 1993 was the year of the 'Baby Bombers' and none of those kids had been involved in anything like it.

Melbourne is the sports capital of Australia. We hold the record for the most people to attend a rugby league state-of-origin match – not bad for a state that, at the time, had no real connection to rugby. Motorcycle racing, the Australian Open tennis, the Grand Prix: bring it to Melbourne and we'll get involved. But none of these sports seems to create the frenzy that an AFL Grand Final does, and 1993 was no exception.

The Friday before the big game was the traditional Grand Final parade through the streets of Melbourne. That year it started at the Arts Centre on St Kilda Road and finished about

Big occasions

a kilometre away on centre stage at Melbourne Central. When we gathered at the Arts Centre the young guys stayed huddled together for support, talking quietly amongst themselves, while we seasoned campaigners laughed and joked with the public and each other. The time came for us to get into the open-top cars that would carry us along the main streets of football-mad Melbourne. As the procession started, the older players were waving, smiling and acknowledging the good-natured taunts from the crowd, while the younger guys – David Calthorpe, Mark Mercuri, Dustin Fletcher, Joe Misiti, Ricky Olarenshaw, James Hird and so on – sat with their heads bowed, only waving occasionally.

We've all seen time-lapse photography on documentaries showing flowers unfurling in the early morning ready to face the heat of the day. That's as closely as I can describe the change that came over the young guys as the parade rolled on. They started shy and coy, looking at their feet and waving in the vague general direction of the crowd, but as the caravan rolled on, they opened up. The transformation was remarkable. They began waving, pointing, cheering, bending over to take kisses from girls who ran alongside the cars, giving phone numbers and taking them – it was amazing. They went from guys who looked like they were heading down the last mile to the electric chair, to guys skipping down the yellow brick road. There was a fear that some of them might injure themselves through sheer exuberance, and they were eventually reined in by some of the more experienced campaigners and settled down.

When we arrived at the shopping centre to be introduced to the crowd, Kevin Sheedy pulled us all to one side and said he had noticed how much we'd enjoyed the experience, but he didn't want anyone getting too carried away. He asked that anyone who had received a note from a member of the crowd hand it over and get their minds back on the job of winning a premiership. 'Don't worry,' he said reassuringly. 'You'll get them back afterwards.'

Reluctantly, good-luck cards, congratulatory notes, break-a-leg (literally) messages and, of course, phone numbers were handed in.

The guys concerned have since complained that those notes and messages were never returned. And consequently, Kev's little black book is the most sought-after in the southern hemisphere.

FAKING IT

ONE OF THE greatest achievements and honours in league football is to be chosen to play for your state. It's fair to say, though, that at times state-of-origin football hasn't been embraced with enthusiasm by the coaches of local sides. It means disruption to their schedule and, of course, the ever-present risk of one of their key players getting injured.

In 1986, in a home-and-away game at Waverley, I received a heavy knock and fell, injuring my elbow. It was very painful and there were concerns that I had dislocated it, or perhaps even chipped the bone. X-rays revealed some short-term damage to nerves, which would probably take a few days to come good. Essendon were playing Hawthorn the following Saturday and during the week I also had state training for an upcoming game against South Australia. The Vics were being coached by none other than Kevin Sheedy.

The club doctors made up a plaster cast for my arm to protect the elbow from knocks and Sheeds, always the tactician, said I had to wear it at state team functions. There would be Hawthorn players there, and he thought it would lead them to believe that perhaps I wouldn't be fit for our game against them.

I never argued with Sheeds, so I did what I was told. When I arrived at the state training meeting I was overwhelmed by everyone's reaction: they all wanted to know how my arm

Faking it

was. Selectors E.J. Whitten and Bobby Skilton, in particular, were very concerned, and it was difficult for me to lie to them. About the only people who didn't sympathise were Hawthorn's Robert DiPierdomenico and Dermott Brereton. Dipper would walk past and 'accidentally' bump me and laugh, saying things like, 'Pity you won't be playing against us this Saturday, Fish – I was so looking forward to knocking you out.'

Carrying on the ruse was particularly tough because, as anyone who has worn one will know, casts aren't all that comfortable. My arm was itchy and I was also dying to straighten it out, which I could easily have done because there was nothing actually wrong with it by that stage. I was constantly disappearing into the toilet to take the cast off, straighten my arm and give it a bit of a scratch. At one stage E.J. asked if I had a bit of gastro as well as a crook elbow.

After the meeting we all went to a compulsory team-building night at the cinema. Sitting next to me was Dipper, and in front of me was Sheeds, who is one of those people who takes a heap of stuff into the movies. Being a coach, he's the only one who can afford it. He was armed with Jaffas, chips, a large soft drink and a bag of assorted lollies. (I know the CSIRO do great work in research into all sorts of things, but why is it they haven't bothered trying to come up with noiseless chip packets and lolly wrappers? Imagine the publicity they would receive, not to mention world adulation and a possible Nobel prize.)

So the lights went down and everyone got settled. About halfway through the movie my arm got itchy, so I quietly took the cast off. Fifteen minutes or so later, hunger got the better of me and I leaned forward and took a handful of Kev's Jaffas. Kev reacted by grabbing my arm and flicking it backwards. The inertia carried it upwards and I clocked Dipper just under the eye. He yelled out at the top of his voice, 'The cast! The bastard's not wearing a cast! He's been fudging!'

Big occasions

I quickly wriggled my arm back in to the plaster as E.J. came over to see what all the ruckus was. He glared at Sheeds and me and then, tongue in cheek, said to Dipper, 'Don't be stupid, Dipper. Of course Paul isn't fudging. No player or coach would abuse the honour of playing state football just to unsettle his local opposition. It wouldn't happen.'

I'm happy to say that my arm made a miraculous recovery very soon after, and the next time I faced training it was as good as gold. History shows, too, that we were beaten by Hawthorn that weekend.

The irony in this tale is that when it came to elbows in league football, Dipper was the foremost expert. He used his to great effect on the opposition throughout his illustrious career!

PILES

A LOT OF people will comment on the honour of playing for your state, and it *is* fantastic. However, it's not all beer and skittles. When you play state football you end up on a team with guys who the previous week were your opposition and trying to knock your block off.

In the early 1990s I was playing for Victoria in Perth and ended up sharing a room with an opposition player, who shall remain nameless. During the stay he was suffering from a very nasty, painful case of piles, so much so that he called the team doctor up to look at them. (I read somewhere a few years ago that scientists have discovered that the oil from pine cones is excellent for soothing piles. I often wonder how they discover things like that. Perhaps there was a scientist working late one night, all alone in the lab. He started to entertain himself with his pants down and a pine cone in his hand, when two other scientists walked in. He stammered, 'It's not what you think. Um . . . um . . . I think I've found a cure for haemorrhoids!')

Anyway, the doctor duly arrived and proceeded to get out his gear. I went to leave, but he grabbed my arm and said, 'No, Fish, you stay. I might need you.' This wasn't what I wanted. Knowing an opposition player had piles was already too much information, but staying while the doctor tended to them was

Big occasions

beyond the pale. However, this week he was my teammate, so I didn't really have much choice.

The patient removed his shorts and rolled over onto his stomach. You can usually tell when something's bad by the reaction of the expert you call in to look at it. For example, nothing scares me more than when a mechanic lifts the bonnet of my car and says, 'This doesn't look good,' or when I get a plumber out and he just shakes his head and says, 'This might take a while.' In this case, I knew things weren't okay when the doctor reeled back and said, 'F--- me! These aren't piles – they're mountains!' I had a look too, and he was right. The only things missing were a couple of sherpas and Edmund Hillary's grandson climbing the south face. No wonder the player couldn't run – I'm surprised he could even walk.

The doc told me to pass the instruments he asked for. He started with a scalpel and then proceeded to tell me exactly what he was doing. 'Now, Paul, I'm just isolating the offending haemorrhoid . . .'

'That's enough info, Doc. I'm here to help, not to learn,' I said quickly. The doctor shrugged and went about his business, while I held my breath. 'It won't take long,' I thought. 'Just a quick nick and I'm out of here. That's all. It won't take long.'

Eventually the procedure was over and everything had been cut, stitched and put away. I went into the corner and sat sucking my thumb until it was time to go to the ground. I've never been able to eat grapes since.

LIKE GOLD

ONE OF THE hassles of Grand Final week for anyone working in footy is people contacting you to try and get tickets to the match. It can actually be quite amusing: any flimsy excuse is enough. I've had people I went to primary school with, who I haven't seen for twenty-five years and who I had nothing to do with at school, ring to try and renew our old acquaintanceship to get tickets. I've had calls from people who once talked to me in passing in Myer. I even had someone phone me whose only link was that they once travelled in the same carriage as me when I caught a train from school to a part-time job – and that was before I was even playing for Essendon!

The best story of people trying to get tickets happened to a colleague of mine at Hawthorn. His phone rang three days before the Grand Final and the conversation went like this.

'Hi, it's Brian,' said the caller.

'Brian?'

'Yes – Brian. We met about eight years ago.'

'Really?'

'Yes.'

'I'm sorry – look, I honestly don't remember you. You'll have to remind me.'

'Remember when you first started playing full-on senior games?'

Big occasions

'Yes.'

'And you played in Sydney one week?'

'Yes.'

'And instead of staying the night, you came home on the last flight out?'

'Yes.'

'And you found your girlfriend in bed with another guy, and you dragged him from the bed and said if you caught him around her again you'd give him a real hard time?'

'Yes...'

'Well, I'm that guy – and I was wondering if there was any chance of a couple of tickets to the Grand Final.'

Needless to say, the caller didn't get any tickets, but the fact that he was prepared to risk life and limb for them shows just how hard they are to get and what lengths people will go to.

PART 8
LIVELIHOOD

TOUR GUIDE

ONE OF THE joys of being in the travel and hospitality industry is witnessing the positive effect your packages can have on people. My company, Journey Events Travel, has been getting fans closer to their favourite sports for over ten years and it still never ceases to amaze me how people can't get enough of any experience that takes them 'inside' the action. (No, we don't trade in used underwear!)

One of the most enjoyable elements of our group packages is visiting club change rooms the morning after a Friday night game. You can still sense the occasion and, unfortunately, you can still smell it as well. But the fans love it.

A few years ago I was hosting a group from Mildura who loved the Bombers and were eagerly awaiting their tour of the MCG's inner sanctum. In the rooms I was busy telling them where certain blokes get changed, how James Hird sits here and reads the *Footy Record*, how Gavin Wanganeen would always have a sleep under those lockers, how Mark Harvey would take the form guide to the toilets (or that's what he told us it was, anyway) and so on, when I spied a woman slipping away from the back of the group. She bent over to pick up what looked like some dirty ankle tape (used to strap players' ankles before they go onto the ground). I was curious, so I approached and asked what she was doing cleaning the rooms, as there are contractors who get paid very well for that duty.

She looked at me incredulously and said, 'But this belongs to Gavin Wanganeen! I'm taking it home to show my sister.'

I couldn't believe it. All I could say was, 'No worries – why not?' I didn't have the heart to tell her that we always had tape fights after a game and it could easily have been a trainer's piece of tape.

ON ANOTHER OCCASION my old mate Mark Harvey was doing the hosting. It was his job to do pretty much what I usually did: show the fans around and give them some insight into the inner workings of an AFL team.

I inquired later from my man on the spot, Tony, as to how it had gone. He began laughing so much he was soon crying, and I couldn't get two words out of him. Slightly worried, I said, 'Calm down and tell me what happened.'

He began to relay the story of how Harvs had walked the group through all the small rooms, such as the doctor's room and the property room, before arriving at the shower block. This was uncharted territory – we hadn't gone there before as we'd never considered that anyone would be interested in the showers. I mean, I could understand people wanting to wash, but not until they got home.

Now Harvey in a shower block full of people is a scary thought, a bit like Mark Mercuri in a room full of women: no one is safe. (Only kidding.) Concerned, I asked Tony, 'What did he say? Was it all right? Is everyone okay?'

Tour guide

Tony paused before replying, 'Oh, it was good actually. He just said that this is where we drop the soap and the boys get up one another.'

Seeing my livelihood fly out the window, I asked, 'And the group?'

'They loved it,' Tony said, much to my relief. I guess there's nothing like a good shower scene to fire people up. All the same, I've never asked Harvs to host again, just in case.

FOOT IN MOUTH

EVER ASKED A slightly overweight woman when she's due, only to get the response, 'I'm not pregnant'?

Ever asked someone, 'How's your dad?' only to be told, 'He's dead'?

Ever said to a group how you would hate to go to a certain place for a holiday because it's a bit of a hole, only to find out someone in the group has a holiday home there?

Ever been asked by a woman to guess her age on her birthday and picked a number ten years too many?

I've done all of the above. Yes, I am afflicted with a disease that chooses its sufferers carefully and spares them nothing in terms of embarrassment and humiliation. Its name? Footinmouthitis.

One such occasion, which I won't forget in a hurry, was when I owned a health club in Glen Waverley and was doing the late shift. This shift was my favourite, as the patrons at that time of night tended to be young and enjoying the social element of belonging to a gym. Sometimes the late-night patrons were society's unfortunates – those to whom life had dealt a harsher hand and who used their membership as a source of escape and for a sense of belonging – or dads who were quite obviously using their membership as a leave pass from home. No matter who they were, I enjoyed their company and saw

Foot in mouth

the club as an ongoing soap opera of real life that, at times, made me feel better about my own.

One of the real positives of joining a club of any sort is that you can share your troubles and woes with the poor sucker behind the counter. In this particular instance, I was that poor sucker.

Two young blokes and I were enjoying chatting about the pros and cons of Lycra getting caught in cracks, and headbands and wristbands heading the way of the dodo, when I thought it time to share with them a little fashion tragedy of sorts. It concerned another member, who belonged to the aforementioned 'unfortunates' category. Remember, this was coming from me – a bloke who thought he looked good in white sneakers with his tracksuit tucked into his socks, and a T-shirt so tight it caused hyperventilation.

I proceeded to tell them of a guy – let's call him 'Roly' – who came to the gym at least four times a week and always wore the same thing. Facing my audience and with my back to the entry door, I described Roly from head to toe, not only detailing his attire but also adding, for colour and effect, its condition and the odours emanating from it. I remember the outfit well, for some reason: white sneakers (says a lot about my choices), brown socks, matching brown Stubbies shorts and, to cap it off, a brown penguin polo shirt.

The boys were loving it, but I couldn't help noticing that their eyes began drifting left of me while I spoke in graphic detail of this loyal and respected member. As I was on a roll, it didn't occur to me why I might be failing to hold their full and undivided attention. But as their eyes began to track left more often while they were still laughing with gusto, I just had to see what was distracting them.

As I turned, everything went into slow motion, like the arrow in the movie *Robin Hood: Prince of Thieves*. It became painfully obvious who else was enjoying the story. There was

Roly, looking himself up and down and probably wishing he had changed his jocks that week. His eyes met mine, and my mind went a million miles an hour trying to work out a way of getting out of this one. I stuttered and muttered something like, 'Hey Roly, good to see you. You may have just heard me speaking about Bob.'

Well, Roly's dress sense and hygiene might have been in question, but his intelligence wasn't. He was quick to retort, 'At least I don't tuck my pants into my socks.'

Touché. It was a hard way to learn a lesson: stop tucking in my trackies.

BRICKS AND MORTAR

FOOTBALL THESE DAYS is a highly professional game. Players are well rewarded for their endeavours, and as a payback, the club expects them to concentrate all their efforts on being professional footballers. It wasn't always like that, though. In the early 1990s many players still had full-time jobs outside the game, not only to supplement their football income, but to give them some options if their playing career were to end.

The best job to have was with an employer who was sympathetic to the fact that you were a league footballer who needed to arrange his work schedule around his playing commitments. I was lucky enough to get a job with Nubrik, one of Essendon's sponsors, represented by two very successful, very large Italian pavers, Tony and Jim. They were only too happy to accommodate any customer who chose to be late paying for their pavers with the threat of physical harm, including to members of the customer's family. In the whole time I was working for them, not one builder – and builders are notoriously bad payers – ever went longer than thirty days on an account.

My job was to sell paving and build business in the northwestern suburbs of Melbourne. When I started, they told me my office would be located at Windy Hill. I imagined that meant I would be in one of the air-conditioned offices up above the social club, but it wasn't to be. I ended up in a 4-metre-long plywood caravan on blocks in the corner of the car park, surrounded by sample patches of paving.

My office was a source of great delight to my teammates. I am a very tall man, and caravans are built by short people for short people. If I wanted to stand upright, I had to raise the skylight in the middle of the van and then stand very still. It must have looked quite bizarre. Anyone wandering past would have seen just the top of my head poking out, like a jack-in-the-box. At one end of the caravan there was a tiny table with benches at each side. If I sat on one of the benches, my legs would tangle in the legs of the table and my knees would get caught.

I have a friend who used to holiday every Christmas with his parents in a very similar van. They would tow it to San Remo, down near Phillip Island, and stay for the summer. He and his sister would sleep on bunks at one end, and every night his mum and dad would collapse the table, put a mattress on it and sleep there. In the morning they'd get up and reset the table, then at night go through the whole procedure again. One night my mate couldn't sleep and was lying quietly in his bed when he heard his parents getting to know each other just a little better. As a kid it's bad enough when you know your parents are 'doing it' without actually catching them at it. For the rest of the holiday he refused to eat at the table. The trauma was just too much, and even when he visited me at my office, he refused to come inside. We had to go into the social club.

The greatest laugh for my teammates was to watch me coming out of the van. You know those nature documentaries where you see a joey emerge from its mother's pouch? The legs come out first, then it twists its shoulders and the head emerges, then it sort of staggers across the ground before bounding off. That's what it was like every time I left my

Bricks and mortar

office. In hindsight, I think Tony and Jim planned it that way: it was so uncomfortable that I spent most of my time on the road making sales calls.

My employers had warned me that the job wouldn't be easy, that builders were difficult to work with and very reluctant to accept change, but they said that if I applied myself and worked hard I could very quickly become the number-one sales rep in the north-western area. This wasn't difficult, as I was the only rep in the north-western area. But I studied my product and soon knew everything there was to know about paving and pavers. There was nothing those builders could ask me that I wouldn't be able to answer.

Armed with all my knowledge, I went to my first appointment with a builder and crapped on for fifteen minutes, not giving the guy a chance. I talked about the different types of pavers, the various ways you could lay them, their carrying capacity and ease of laying, and how good the finished product would look. I went on and on, like Forrest Gump's army mate going on about shrimps and shrimp boats. Finally I stopped to draw breath and then, as a closer, asked, 'Okay. Now I've got my tape – how about if I measure up and give you a quote?'

The builder just looked at me and said, 'Concrete's cheaper,' and walked back to what he was doing.

This happened time and time again, and for a while that goal of number-one sales rep in the north-west looked like eluding me. I decided that perhaps it was time to change tack and hone my skills on the domestic market. Eventually I got a call for my first domestic quote, from an elderly couple who wanted an estimate of the cost of putting down a path from their back door to the clothesline. I arrived with my tape measure, measuring wheel, three forests' worth of brochures and more confidence than Shane Crawford at a players' revue. I bamboozled them with product knowledge and the multitude of ways pavers could be used around the house. Eventually, through what those in the trade call suggestive selling, I up-sold them from a 4-metre path to a driveway, entertainment area, side way and barbecue.

I took the measurements back to Tony and Jim to work out the quote and it came to just under $14 000. They said I was a cold, callous and calculating operator who had taken advantage of an old couple who just needed a paved area to keep their shoes dry when they hung the washing out . . . They were so proud of me.

That night guilt overtook me and the next day I decided to return to the clients' house and unravel the mess I'd made. When I arrived, rather than being stoned and abused I was welcomed like the prodigal son. Overnight they had looked at my ideas and decided that everything I had come up with was great. It took me three hours, half a homemade chocolate cake, six jam fancies and three cups of coffee to talk them out of getting it all done. In fact, at one stage they threatened to go to someone else to get the work done if I wasn't prepared to do it. I worked harder to talk them out of it than I had talking them into it.

The look on their faces when I left was quite quizzical, and I'm sure all of us sat down at home that night and thought, 'What the hell happened today?'

THE SYNDICATE

THEY SAY FIRST impressions are lasting impressions, and my first impression of the horse-racing industry is probably a good reason why I have never become a racehorse owner.

I was only a kid kicking a lot of goals way back in 1984 when I was approached by a bloodstock agency to head up a promotion for them, which was designed to put together a syndicate to buy and race a horse. The deal was pretty straightforward: I would get a free ride and share in the winnings, if any, while the other members of the syndicate would each pay an upfront fee and monthly maintenance. It sounded like a bit of fun, and I had a lot of faith in the men behind it, so I thought, 'Why not?'

It took only a few days to sell all the available spots in the syndicate, and everyone involved was over the moon. We had a get-to-know-you night, where we named our horse (I can't remember what it was – let's run with 'Bomber Flyer') and had a few drinks with the people we would be standing next to on the podium when we received the Melbourne Cup a few years down the track. There was lots of optimism, and naivety to match. We partied till late, sharing stories of previous experiences in racing and hopes of being first-time lucky. They were a great group of people, who were genuinely in it for the fun and the social aspects. We all

Livelihood

left agreeing that the next time we caught up would be at our new horse's first trial.

A couple of weeks later I got an excited phone call from the representative at the bloodstock agency – let's call him 'Ron'. 'Fish, you're not going to believe what happened this morning!' Ron said.

'What, mate?' I replied.

'Bomber Flyer won his first trial by ten lengths and looks a champion in the making!' he screeched.

'That's great – but weren't the syndicate members meant to be notified so we could all get out there to see it?'

'Yeah, sorry, mate, but it was put together at the last moment. Next time, hey.' I must admit to being pretty happy about the news, and said I would look forward to the next opportunity to see Bomber Flyer in a trial. There was no reason to doubt Ron at the time, so I put the incident behind me.

A few weeks later I had another phone call from a very excited Ron. 'Fish, Bomber Flyer just had another run and streeted the field by about six lengths!'

'You're kidding,' I said.

'No, it was amazing, mate. I reckon we've got a gun on our hands!' Ron was stoked and told me about the trial from start to finish.

'But what about the phone call to let me know about the run?' I inquired.

'I'm really sorry, mate, but most of the time these things aren't planned. I'll do my best next time, okay?' Not much I could do other than to say I really wanted to know the next time the horse was running and I'd be very disappointed if he didn't ring.

It was only about a week later that his next call came through. Bomber Flyer had won again, by an incredible seven lengths this time, and everyone was convinced he was the reincarnation of Phar Lap. Again, no invitation to witness these

The syndicate

feats had been forthcoming, and my enthusiasm was starting to be clouded by some doubts. My requests to Ron to visit the stables were met with absolute assurances that I must get out there, but whenever I suggested a time it was unfortunately 'inconvenient' for someone there.

Another call, and another victory to Bomber Flyer by a big margin in his final trial before racing in a country meet, had Ron almost jumping through the phone in his excitement at the horse's potential. It was easy to see how intoxicating the industry could be if you were lucky enough to get on a winner. I couldn't wait to see this money-making machine in the flesh, and our syndicate was counting its future millions.

But there's nothing like getting ahead of yourself. A few days later another call came through from Ron, only this one had a different tone. It went something like this.

'That you, Paul?' a subdued Ron asked.

'Yeah, it's me. What's wrong?'

'After Bomber Flyer's last trial he pulled up a bit sore, so we put him out to spell him.'

'Good idea,' I said.

'We thought so too,' came the reply.

'What's wrong, Ron?' (Try saying that ten times fast.)

'Bomber Flyer got bitten by a snake last night and is dead,' Ron muttered.

'Dead?' I said, in disbelief.

'Yeah, there was nothing we could do, mate.'

'I can't believe it. So what now, Ron?'

'Well, we'll bury Bomber Flyer and get you guys a new horse, I reckon,' was his response. I could hardly believe what I was hearing. Having never even seen Bomber Flyer, there was no use asking to view the body as it could have been any old horse. I really felt for the rest of the syndicate members, who'd had their future hopes hanging on this next big thing.

Livelihood

Call me sentimental, but I would like to think that Bomber Flyer never really died and in fact had a name change to something like 'Black Knight' or some other champion of the 1980s. It's just a way of coping for me, I suppose, and trying to move on from one of the most traumatic experiences an animal lover can have. And it's a better option than thinking he was turned into a can of Pal dog food.

PART 9
COMEBACK

TWILIGHT ZONE

A FEW MONTHS ago Jo and the kids went away, and my parents invited me over for dinner. Dad, Mum and I shared a few wines and I decided it was probably safer to stay the night than to drive home. I had to sleep on the fold-out in my old room. All my stuff had long gone (in fact, the minute I was out of sight on the day I left home, Mum had a garage sale), and it felt quite weird sleeping there. It was home, all the surroundings were home, but it felt a little like I didn't really belong. Of course, next morning Mum came into my room like she used to when I was a kid, threw open the curtains and cried, 'Breakfast's ready!' I knew I couldn't have been anywhere else, but just the same, it was a bit disconcerting.

Going back to the Essendon Footy Club in 2002 was a little like that. Getting myself mentally and physically ready to play league football again after eighteen months of low-intensity domesticity was one thing, but going back to a place I had made my home for fifteen years before leaving for six years to play for Hawthorn was quite another. It was always going to be weird, but I didn't think it would be *that* weird.

I wasn't prepared for my first encounter with the place I once knew so well. Arriving at Windy Hill, I pulled up out the front of what used to be Mrs C's milk bar but is now a health clinic. Change number one: milk bar – health clinic. Like old times, I parked out the front and headed in. I didn't realise the area was now a one-hour zone, and I copped a fine on my first night. Someone was going to pay dearly for giving me no warning.

I strode across the road, turned to face the club rooms and made my way towards what used to be the front door. It was no longer there and I wandered around like the big boy lost (brother of little) until a supporter showed me how to get in. This was great: I already knew a lot of supporters were thinking, 'He's too old, he's too slow', and now here was one thinking, 'He's too stupid. If he can't find his way in, how's he going to find the ball in a pack?'

There was rubbish everywhere, as there were renovations taking place. I headed to my old locker area, only to find it wasn't there. The locker room was now so big you could get lost in it, and they had a squat rack (for leg workouts) where my locker used to be! This wasn't the homecoming I'd hoped for; talk about subtle hints. I was taken aback by the changes and a little embarrassed about not recognising much. But as the rooms started to fill and teammates old and new came over and made me feel welcome, I realised that six years away may have changed the appearance of the place, but not the feel of it. It turned out to be like putting on that old pair of trackies you've had in the wardrobe for years, to find they still fit like a glove (unless you've been on the donut diet!).

Before long the unfamiliar surroundings were forgotten and I was being swept along with the rest of the team and getting into the task before me. I decided the best thing to do was forget about easing my way in, and just get on with it. I quickly applied myself to working out the lie of the land: which players thought they had the power, which ones actually did have the power, and who were the next wave. Training was both a lot of hard work and a lot of fun as I set out to make new friends and re-establish myself as an Essendon player.

Twilight zone

The summer went quicker than I thought it would – funny how that is the case with advancing age – and it wasn't long before we had our first practice match in February. I had a minor calf injury and didn't play, instead sitting on the sidelines riding an exercise bike. I wasn't too worried, as the season was still a fair way off and it wasn't as if Kevin had any intention of playing me at that point anyway.

Post-match, Sheeds was giving his review to the boys and I was overcome by an overwhelming feeling that nothing had changed. The message was all too familiar: *older players should look out, as young players would be given every chance; don't get comfortable, your position's up for grabs*, etc., etc. I bent down to whisper in James Hird's ear that I was caught in a time warp. We caught Kevin's attention and he gave me a long glare as if to say, 'I know what you're thinking, but keep it to yourself.'

Anyway, I thought it might be nice to record here some of my observations from 2002, which was for me a season spent in a twilight zone of sorts, where things had changed, but not really. Or maybe it was just me. Or maybe it's that stuff I've been smoking . . . never mind. Here are some of the things I noticed:

- Sheeds had got a personal assistant, which meant that at least he had someone telling him where he should be at any given time on any given day. It didn't mean he'd be there; it just meant he knew he should be there.
- Matthew Lloyd had started carrying a 'Bullworker' in his bag for impromptu body touch-ups. I had to ask him where his private locker room was – I couldn't imagine him getting changed and showering with the masses.
- Hirdy had screwed a small bell to his locker so he could ring it when he needed Adi, the property steward, to bring him his boots or take away his dirty jumper, or fan him if he was too hot.

- Paul Barnard's locker was the only one without a mirror – which is a cruel irony, because to be honest he was one of the few who really needed one.
- Sean Wellman had developed a corduroy fetish and seemed to be celebrating National Bad Shirt Day every day.
- Mark 'Spike' McVeigh was obviously a hair-product salesman, because in his locker he had everything you could ever need for your hair.
- Mark Johnson liked the sound of his own voice so much he would often talk himself to sleep.
- Adam Ramanauskas never brushed his hair for fear of more falling out.
- Scotty Lucas wouldn't even pass the soap in the shower.
- And Steve Alessio spent as much time grooming the hair on his chest as he did the hair on his head.

About the only thing that hadn't changed since I'd left was Mark Harvey's haircut. I often wonder if he cuts it himself. (I can't for the life of me understand those people at Breville who, every Father's Day, advertise the home haircut kit. Who in their right mind, apart from Harvs, would cut their own hair? And realistically, are you going to trust the daughter you just grounded to cut it for you? I don't think so.)

As unfair as all the above might sound, as cheap a shot as every observation might be, as low as they are, gee, it feels better to have written them down!

And as far as I was concerned? Well, apart from the odd obsessive compulsive disorder for looking after my own footy gear, who's perfect?

ROUTINE

THINK ABOUT THAT afternoon on your big overseas trip when you were in a London pub and the lagers were flowing pretty well. You struck up a conversation with a couple of Brits and in your drunken state said, 'No, really, when you come to Australia, you must stay with me.'

Twelve months later there's a knock on your door and there they are, having taken you at your word. After a few months you have to ask them to leave, but it's not until they've gone that you realise just how much of your time and space they've been taking up.

That's what it's like giving up football. It's only after you give it away that you realise the time and effort not only you, but the rest of your family, have been putting into it. Everything you have been doing for so long – in my case, twenty-nine years – stops, just like that.

A lot of retired players have trouble adjusting to not playing the game and not being around the team environment. The AFL and the Players Association have realised this and now have various strategies in place to address the issue. They conduct workshops and have discussions, and before players leave a club they are counselled on what to expect. Every Thursday they get past players together for a chat, and then for old times' sake make them all shower together before going home.

(Well, they do try to make sure you don't sleep with a footy under your pillow.)

I didn't realise how regimented my life was when I was playing: *Do this. Do that. Be here at a certain time. Be there when we tell you. Don't eat that. Don't go there. Sorry, you can't go out – you have to be in bed early before the big game.* It goes on and on, and when you're part of it you just accept it. It's when you stop that it all falls over.

For example, I was out in the backyard a few weeks ago and Jo needed me to come inside for dinner. She had to dress one of the kids in a green tracksuit and send them out with a message: 'Dinner's ready, and you should come and sit on the bench and rest for a few minutes.'

Not quite, but it hasn't been easy to adjust to family life. Jo and the kids had managed quite well without me home for dinner a few nights a week, or on weekends. I get in their way now, and Jo swears she has four kids to get organised on a Saturday, rather than three.

We've all had to make adjustments. Thursday night, for instance, is the night the teams are announced. When you're playing, if you get picked you go to a meeting and receive your instructions for the game. Now, purely out of habit, I find myself asking Jo on a Thursday what to expect on the weekend. She knows I'm used to specific instructions, so occasionally she'll draw a diagram on the fridge whiteboard of me in the car, with arrows and times to pick up and drop off the kids. (Don't laugh – it works.)

There are some Saturday mornings I'll get my kitbag out and just stare at it. Nine times out of ten this behaviour results in the kids edging away, making circles near their ear with their finger as they shut the door and run to their mum.

Mondays are a bit weird, too. I still find it difficult not to go through the papers to find out how the football critics think I played. I made the big mistake one recent Monday

Routine

morning of asking Jo to rate my performance over the weekend. I'll never do that again – gee, you women can be cruel when you want to be.

LAST HURRAH

AT TEAM MEETINGS during my final season, I sat up the back of Essendon's magnificent players' auditorium to ensure I had full vision of everyone and everything. That seat also meant that when the lights went out, fewer people would see me nod off. My partner in crime at the back of the room was Spike McVeigh, a young man totally confused about what to do with his hair and, worse still, what to wear in order to look cool. I did my best to nurse him through these troubled times but obviously to no avail, as he has continued to defy fashion logic.

Team meetings had long ago lost their magic for me and I struggled to maintain a conscious state. Nothing personal against assistant coach Mark Harvey, who produced some riveting video highlights with barely intelligible commentary from himself, but I was weary from the physical demands of the modern footballer.

Actually, it was as boring as bat shit. If I wasn't sleeping (which Spike unfailingly brought to everyone's attention), there was plenty to entertain me. I don't want to give the wrong impression, but twenty years of the same ol', same ol' can develop more than a touch of cynicism in anyone.

The club, in fact, went out of its way to freshen things up for the players, and there was no greater example of this than

Last hurrah

what happened during the run into the finals and September itself. First, assistant coach John Quinn dug up a truly uninspiring video on the great British decathlete Daley Thompson. By the end of it the boys were virtually catatonic, with most of those still awake trying to work out if their parents had been alive when Daley was at his peak. Personally, I found it an inspired choice.

Next, we were paid a surprise visit by Tony Liberatore, a man whom most of the players had viewed with a deal of animosity during his playing days, but also a man for whom everyone held a grudging respect for the way he'd carved out a magnificent career. Libba spoke about taking opportunities and not wasting your time in football. If he could have that long a career in the game, with all he'd had to contend with, then anyone could.

The first week of the finals came and who should be in town promoting his new book but the Crocodile Hunter himself, Steve Irwin. Somehow a tenuous link between Steve and the club had been found: it turned out he'd lived near Windy Hill when he was a toddler and actually barracked for the Bombers. He bowled into the auditorium, larger than life, with a big 'Crikey!' to kick it off. The boys loved him and got right into it.

He started to speak about how his great-grandfather and grandfather had gone to World War I together and how – at least, this is what I could make of his speech – they fought that war so we could be sitting here today playing Australian Rules, the greatest game in the world. It was a powerful message that was somehow compromised by Steve's tendency to throw in way too much colour and way too many 'crikeys'. He lost his place a bit but it was great to have him there, as some of the players were big fans. He was larger than life and I thought, 'If this is an act, he does a great job keeping it up all the time.' His appearance turned out to be a good omen,

Comeback

as we went on to defeat West Coast at Colonial Stadium on the Saturday night.

That game also turned out to be what I feel was a type of 'cleansing' for myself and the Essendon supporters. Late in the last quarter I was playing forward after a long night on the ball when somehow it landed in my lap, which meant I only had to turn and kick it through for a goal. I managed to execute this manoeuvre with a minimum of fuss and thrust my arms into the air in joy and disbelief, when all of a sudden I felt a pain like someone had shot me in the leg. I fell to the ground, laughing at how ridiculous I must look. It turned out to be only cramp, but the timing couldn't have been worse, as everyone's attention was on me. Teammates came in to pick me up and we all had a bit of a laugh, the goal having put the game comfortably in our keeping.

The runner made his anticipated appearance to request my presence on the bench, and I must admit it was the only time in my career that I was pleased to get dragged. I still had a big, slightly embarrassed grin on my face as I made my way towards the boundary. What happened as I was going off will live forever in my memory: the Essendon supporters gave me an overwhelming ovation. Short of winning the premiership, it made the whole year worthwhile and was the ultimate way to say goodbye to a group of people with whom I had shared a mixed relationship.

Without that moment, the day in 1995 when I got booed off in my second-last game for Essendon would have been the way a lot of people remembered my career at the Bombers. This occasion in 2002 was symbolic, in that they seemed to be telling me my efforts were appreciated and my comeback had given us both a second chance. That's what I would like to believe, anyway.

Surviving another week into the finals, albeit without Hirdy and Dustin Fletcher due to injury and suspension

Last hurrah

respectively, meant we had another guest speaker to look forward to. Confronting the daunting task of having to beat Port Adelaide in Adelaide, we were in need of some serious motivation. How were they going to top Daley, Libba and the Croc Hunter? Well, my concerns proved unfounded when, on Thursday night, in walked comedian extraordinaire and my personal favourite, Dave Hughes. Unfortunately Dave couldn't provide the required motivation, as he prefers to tell jokes for a living. Although we did laugh ourselves into stitches, the great man can now lay claim to being responsible for our demise in Adelaide that week. I guess he wasn't very motivational, but he was definitely a highlight.

That loss hit me harder than I thought it would. The realisation that the year was over, mission unaccomplished and final retirement ahead, drew a very emotional response from me. I'm not sure why it was worse than my retirement the first time around. Maybe it was because I knew what to expect – that it would be a brutal cutting-off from all I had known and put so much passion into for well over half a lifetime.

Regardless, it was over. At least I had the footy trip to London to look forward to, where I planned to sign off in appropriate style.

What a year. No regrets and a heap more great memories from a bonus year of football. Don't die wondering!